MANDATED TO
LIVE HOLY

Juanita N. Stallings

Largo, MD

Copyright © 2017 Juanita N. Stallings

All rights reserved under the international copyright law. No part of this book may be reproduced or transmitted in any form or by any means, electronic or mechanical, including photocopying, recording, or by any information storage or retrieval system, without express written permission of the author or publisher. The exception is reviewers, who may quote brief passages for review.

Christian Living Books
P. O. Box 7548
Largo, MD 20792
www.christianlivingbooks.com
We bring your dreams to fruition.

ISBN Paperback 9781562293505
ISBN Electronic Version 9781562293512

Unless otherwise noted, Scripture quotations are taken from the King James Version of the Bible. Scripture quotations marked AMPC are taken from the Amplified Bible®, Copyright © 1954, 1958, 1962, 1964, 1965, 1987 by The Lockman Foundation. Used by permission. www.Lockman.org. Scripture quotations are from the ESV® Bible (The Holy Bible, English Standard Version®), Copyright © 2001 by Crossway, a publishing ministry of Good News Publishers. Used by permission. All rights reserved. Scripture quotations marked (NIV) are taken from the Holy Bible, New International Version®, NIV®, Copyright©1973, 1978, 1984, 2011 by Biblica, Inc® Used by permission of Zondervan. All rights reserved worldwide. www.zondervan.com. Scripture quotations marked NASB are taken from the New American Standard Bible® (NASB), Copyright © 1960, 1962, 1963, 1968, 1971, 1972, 1973,1975, 1977, 1995 by The Lockman Foundation. Used by permission. www.Lockman.org. Scripture quotations marked (NKJV) are taken from the New King James Version. Copyright© 1982 by Thomas Nelson, Inc. Used by permission. All rights reserved. Scripture quotations marked (NLT) are taken from the Holy Bible, New Living Translation, Copyright © 1996, 2004, 2007 by Tyndale House Foundation. Used by permission of Tyndale House Publishers, Inc., Carol Stream, Illinois 60188. All rights reserved.

Printed in the United States of America

CONTENTS

Introduction	....	v
Chapter 1	Holiness	7
Chapter 2	Knowing Who We Really Are	25
Chapter 3	Guarding Your Mind	47
Chapter 4	Guarding Your Heart	61
Chapter 5	Guarding Your Body	75
Chapter 6	Guarding Your Soul	95
Chapter 7	Guarding Your Spirit	109
Chapter 8	The Defeat of Satan	115
Chapter 9	Be Ye Holy for God Is Holy	121
Chapter 10	Promises to God's Children	133
Acknowledgments	....	135
About the Author	....	137

INTRODUCTION

The purpose of this book is to draw God's people back to their rightful place with Him. It's to help them understand the challenges experienced in life and how they can use them to make a difference. Moreover, the contents have been penned to encourage believers to stop running from who they are in the Lord. Have you attempted to disqualify yourself from being the person God has called you to be? Have you done horrible things in your quest to escape God's will? It's time to stop and embrace your unique, authentic self and allow God to live in you so the world can experience the fullness of life because of your existence.

For those who currently have no idea who they really are and are searching for their identity, my prayer is, you will truly come to the knowledge of who you are and who the Enemy is. Most importantly you will discover and experience God. Perhaps, you had such knowledge before but you were tricked out of believing and living it. Alternatively, your main concern and purpose in life may be to fit in and be "normal," instead of being who God called you to be. If you have found yourself in one of these categories. I want to expose the Enemy, his tricks, and tactics that keep you from your true identity which is intended to lead you to your destiny. On the other hand, if you are conscious of your God- given identity, have accepted it and you are holding on by faith, this book will encourage you on your Christian journey and rouse you to fulfill your God-given purpose.

Be ignorant no more! As you read the pages of this book you will forgive and be forgiven; you will be delivered and set free. Discover and embrace who God really called you to be and live it out to the fullest with no apologies.

Chapter 1
....

HOLINESS

Perhaps, you're wondering who I am and what gives me the right to write a book on holiness. Well, I am a young woman of God who knew from an early age that I was called to live holy. However, I had no idea how to do it. I am talking about genuinely living holy, not just appearing to be holy. I was frustrated because I knew how I was supposed to live but I did not know how. Consequently, I experienced several mishaps on my Christian journey. Those mistakes taught me many valuable lessons, which have led to my success on the rest of my Christian journey; I simply desire to share them with you.

My prayer is that my experiences and life lessons will help others who know they have been called to live holy – and even those who don't know this very call is on their lives – to live holy. Maybe, you don't know what holiness is or you just don't understand how to successfully live this lifestyle. I want to help you live as God has called you to. Living holy is not to be done as a chore, duty or obligation but with exceeding joy and happiness. I decided to share with you what I know in good faith. It will help you to live a life of holiness as God intended on your Christian journey.

It always seemed as if I was set apart from the day I was born. I was different. In every group (the majority) and situation, although I found my place, I could always tell that I was different. There was always a distinct difference between me and everyone else in the group or between my situation and their situations. The one thing that I learned was none of these instances were by coincidence. God purposely allowed me to see and feel the contrast between me and everyone else; we are all different. However, God was trying to show me at such a young age that being different was nothing to feel bad, uncomfortable or ashamed of. Far from that, my differentness was unique and was a strength that would help me discover and understand how I differed from the world, my likeness to God, my Father, and His role in my life.

Here's a brief insight of me and where I came from to give you a clearer understanding of what I'm talking about. I have a large family. My mom is one of nine children; her mom is one of ten. Her dad is one of twenty-three. I grew up around family. All of my uncles and aunts were married for as long as I can remember; they all seemed happy and blessed.

However, my mom and dad separated when I was seven and got divorced when I was about ten or eleven. My older brother is the first grandchild on both sides of our family (I never got the chance to meet my grandfather on my father's side; he passed away when my father was 14). I was the first granddaughter on my mom's side and the only granddaughter on my father's side. Needless to say, my brother and I were like the experiment kids. We made the first mistakes and failures and learned the hard way so to speak because we didn't have anybody to learn from. That is, other than our friends who were from an entirely different world and upbringing.

All of my cousins had their moms and dads living at home. Like I said earlier, they appeared to have the ideal family unit. This was the first aspect of my life that made me different. My parents' divorce made me feel like an outcast because my home was no longer what I knew the ideal home to be. It was no longer what I'd seen and once lived before my parents' divorced. From very early, I felt like I had nobody who could relate to me; there was no one to talk to about my situation and life in general. Yes, even as a child, it's important to have someone to talk to about your feelings and what's going on with you. Some people may think what a child is dealing with is trivial and unimportant but it's a big matter to the child. It can have lifelong effects. What I know now, but didn't know then is that the Lord was trying to teach me to look to Him for guidance, counsel, comfort, love, and everything that I needed.

> *For a child is born to us, a son is given to us. The government will rest on his shoulders. And he will be called: Wonderful Counselor, Mighty God, Everlasting Father, Prince of Peace.* (Isaiah 9:6 NLT)

I didn't know who I was or why I was here; my life was so different. Nevertheless, it seemed like all of the elders I came in contact with knew exactly who I was. From as early as I can remember it felt like there wasn't a church service I was in that I didn't receive a word of prophecy about who I was or what I was going to be. I will not assume that everyone reading this has a religious background or that you're familiar with religious terms. For the benefit of those who may not know, a word of prophecy or a prophetic word is the foretelling or prediction of what is to come (*Dictionary.com*). I like to say it's a forth telling of what is to come. The difference between a prophetic word and a psychic's prediction is that a prophetic word generates from God and or a person being used by God to speak for God; it's a foreshadow of your future. However, a psychic's prediction is just that; a prediction from a person or witch being used by Satan (whether the person being used knows it or not).

At first, these prophecies felt good. On hearing them, I thought: "Wow, the Lord is going to do that through me. The Lord is going to give me that. Wow, that's the life I'm going to live. I'm so special." Again, I felt good about these prophecies in the beginning. But when I realized that there would be many, many years before I would see anything close to them coming to pass, the prophecies got more and more annoying. Trying to live holy and waiting on God became more difficult. It felt like I was the only one attempting to live holy. As a matter of fact, it appeared that all of the "normal" people around me were happy and blessed while nothing was happening for me. I wanted to be "normal." Living holy was too hard. What I didn't realize then but do now is that it wasn't that living holy was too hard. The reality was that living holy in this world is; living separated from this world (that to me at the time felt lonely) and because I didn't know how to deal with the feeling of loneliness, made it seem hard.

What I was illuded by like many others was my perception of the blessed life. I thought that having material things and people in my life equated to being blessed. In my mind, having money, fine clothes, gadgets, what appeared to be the American dream, immediate family and things of that nature would make me happy. Now, don't misunderstand me; I had everything I needed – food, clothes, and shelter. However, I didn't have the luxury of having most of the things I wanted. I longed for parents with enough money to buy me stuff and the ideal immediate family, which was lacking after my parents got divorced. As I matured, I discovered that while those things are blessings, not having them doesn't exactly disqualify you from being blessed.

> *But blessed are those who trust in the Lord and have made the Lord their hope and confidence. They are like trees planted along a riverbank, with roots that reach deep into the water. Such trees are not bothered by the heat or worried by long months of drought. Their leaves stay green, and they never stop producing fruit.* (Jeremiah 17:7-8 NLT)

In ignorance because my life was set up differently, I was forced to be blessed! What do I mean? I didn't have a lot of money growing up, and my "American dream immediate family" was taken from me at a young age. Consequently, the lack of those things led me to know God the way I do now. I had no choice but to trust and put all of my hope in Him instead of in money, material things or even family. Would I have the foundational relationship with God that I have now had I not had this childhood experience? I don't know. What I do know is that I'm forever grateful that I developed this relationship. Sometimes, when we look at ourselves in comparison to others, we tend to focus on what others have over us. We really shouldn't look at it that way. God made us all different; He made our situations different as well. God knows exactly what He's doing. Our differences are meant to set us apart, not to make us feel abandoned. They actually show us our likeness to God and the authenticity of ourselves.

Our differences cause us to stand out from the majority. They bring to light what the majority is missing, which can only be identified when we allow our uniqueness to show. In other words, if we try to blend in with the majority, instead of standing out, we will hide the very thing that the majority needs. The differences we possess are assets, not liabilities or things to be ashamed of. When we embrace our uniqueness as the light that draws others, we will permit ourselves to be who we really are in Christ.

> *Therefore, come out from among unbelievers, and separate yourselves from them, says the Lord. Don't touch their filthy things, and I will welcome you. And I will be your Father, and you will be my sons and daughters, says the Lord Almighty.* (2 Corinthians 6:17-18 NLT)

I can remember it like yesterday. It was in my grandparents' living room (where we held most of our church services). My aunt prophesied to me:"The Lord has great things in store for you. He has a great plan and man (husband that is) for you but…you have to remain pure)." I could remember doing cartwheels on the inside: "Oh, wow! God has all of that for me. Oh, yeah! I'm going to do it; I'm going to live pure; I'm not going to mess this up. I want all that God has for me and nothing and no one is going to stop me from getting it." I was about twelve or thirteen at the time but I meant it with all of my heart. However, I didn't understand at that time all that it would take; I didn't even understand the full meaning of living pure. But one thing was certain – though I didn't fully understand how to; I knew I was mandated to live holy.

Maybe, you've had a similar experience. Perhaps, you've known or you were told from a young age that you were different. Not necessarily in those exact words, but you've known or you were told you're special, anointed, God has His hand on you or something of that nature. And if you're anything like I was, you didn't fully understand what that meant. On the other hand, you may never have been told these things or anything like them. However, something deep inside of you always made you feel different. I want to help you understand just what that feeling really is.

I find it necessary to give you this information about me as well as the personal information I'll share about myself in a later chapter for several reasons. First, so you will understand where I am coming from and have a little background information about me. Also, I hope you will not judge me but be reminded that like you, I am human. Another reason is because like you, I didn't always understand why God allowed certain things to happen in my life. But as you will read further in this book you will see, I do understand now. I pray that this book will help you to fit the pieces together and understand your life experiences better than you have thus far.

There are some important things to know when you're mandated to live holy. The first thing is whether you or anyone around you knows who you are. Satan, the enemy does and his most important task is to keep you from knowing who you are. Secondly, the moment that you or someone else recognizes who you are, Satan works on tricking you into believing you're not who you are. Thirdly, to avoid this from happening you have to guard your mind, heart, body, soul, and spirit so that you can know the will of God concerning you and stay in it. And finally; is the must for you to live holy.

From the moment you're born and sometimes, even before then, Satan is working on ways to steal from, kill, and destroy you.

> *The thief cometh not, but for to steal, and to kill, and to destroy: I am come that they might have life, and that they might have it more abundantly.* (John 10:10 KJV)

If you don't know who you are, Satan is pretty subtle with his tricks. Once you or others recognize the hand of God in your life, it's important to stay under the hand of God. In other words, stay in the will of God. The best way to do that is by studying and applying the Word of God to your life, and by fasting and praying. If you don't do these things, you are sure to fall straight into the Enemy's trap every time. It doesn't matter how much you desire in your heart to stay in the will of God; you will fall out of His will if you do not pray, fast and apply His Word to your life. When I received all those prophecies, I thought my heart and will were good enough to keep me. However, although I had the right heart and will, I lacked the power required to be led by my heart and not my flesh. The Word of God warns us about this. If we read and study the Word of God, we can avoid many mishaps on our Christian journey.

> *Watch and pray, that ye enter not into temptation: the spirit indeed is willing, but the flesh is weak.* (Matthew 26:41 KJV)

It's important to mention the prophecies over my life because those said prophecies and the process of waiting for them to be fulfilled led me to my true relationship with God. It was not because I was so hungry for the manifestation of the prophecies. Honestly, as I said earlier, after a while, those prophecies got more and more annoying because I kept hearing them, yet, not seeing them come to pass. So, how did these prophecies lead me to my true relationship with God?

Well, for me, it was annoying to have to wait to get in the presence of a man or woman of God to hear what God had to say to me and the same thing over and over at that (lol). I got so tired of receiving prophetic words that I said to God: "God why don't you just talk to me; I don't want to hear from a prophet. Just tell me what you have to say." Well, for the first time, God told me directly what He had to say; I'll never forget it. He said: "Do you tell your secrets to strangers? I use my prophets to speak to you because they talk to me too – we communicate." Wow! It didn't get any clearer than that for me. Don't get me wrong; men and women of God (Prophets) are essential to our Christian journeys, but we ought not to rely on them only to hear what God has to say to us. Prophets are used to give us fresh words from the Lord. Basically, they are used in this instance to tell us something we did not know. However, as believers, prophets should be used more to confirm what God has already spoken to us personally because unlike the unbelievers, we are in a relationship with God. Therefore, we should not have to rely on prophets to hear from God in general. We should be hearing from Him personally throughout our relationship with Him. What God was saying to me then and what He's saying to you right now is that He wants to talk to you too – directly. God wants a relationship with you, but you have to be willing to be in a relationship with Him for it to work. A one-way relationship isn't a relationship at all.

In essence, that's really what holiness is all about – having a relationship with God. When you desire a relationship with God, you are looking for holiness because God is holy. Most people who don't want to live holy, don't desire a relationship with God; they are ok with religion. They say they have accepted God but lack the passion for getting to know Him more. But God did not create us for religion; He created us for relationship, which I'll talk more about in a later chapter.

As I said, it is very important for men and women of God to be led by the Holy Spirit, to speak the Word of God and to prophesy.

> *But how can they call on him to save them unless they believe in him? And how can they believe in him if they have never heard about him? And how can they hear about him unless someone tells them? And how will anyone go and tell them without being sent? That is why the Scriptures say, "How beautiful are the feet of messengers who bring good news!"* (Romans 10:14-15 NLT)

However, the saints of God (the receivers of the word) have a greater responsibility to take heed to the prophetic word and bathe the Word of God and those prophecies over our lives in prayer (communication with God). We must first remember the word correctly. Yes, I said correctly; we should not make our own interpretations of the word. Rather, we need to receive the word as it is given whether we fully understand it or not. Then we need to seek God daily regarding the prophetic word; this is done through prayer and reading God's Word. When we don't pray for clarity and direction regarding a word of prophecy, we tend to mess up the very thing God wants to do through and for us. We do this because we misinterpret or jump ahead of God's timing concerning the word. As a result, we blame God or call the prophet a false prophet because the prophecy as we interpreted it did not come to pass.

For example, if you receive a word of prophecy that God will use you to minister to the nations, and you take it upon yourself to get your passport and travel all over the world to minister (physically) without seeking God for clarity, you may have missed it. Maybe, God wanted you to write books, produce movies or do something else that would go all over the world and minister to the nations. Who knows how God will fulfill the prophecy over your life? Nobody but God. Therefore, you must continually seek Him concerning every word He speaks to you until that word fully comes to pass. This is also important to do because it's not enough to have a heart to do right concerning the prophecy, to hear the Word of God and receive prophecies. It's so much deeper than that. The Enemy doesn't care about how many prophetic words we hear. He cares and is threatened by how much of that word we apply to our lives. Thus, praying, reading, studying, meditating on, and applying the Word of God to our lives help us take heed and bathe the prophetic words of God we receive over us.

For we know in part, and we prophesy in part. (1 Corinthians 13:9 KJV)

And don't get me started on those who add and subtract from the prophecy (what God is saying). Which again, is why it's so important for you to bathe the prophetic word in prayer; because you don't necessarily want to just take the physical vessel's (the prophet) word as gold. You want to seek God on exactly what he is telling you through the vessel he uses.

Dear friends, do not believe everyone who claims to speak by the Spirit. You must test them to see if the spirit they have comes from God. For there are many false prophets in the world. (1 John 4:1 NLT)

Therefore, in order to understand prophecy over our lives, we must soak it in prayer and continue seeking God to stay in His will concerning it. Understand that when the Lord sends you a prophetic word, it's to let you know what you need to know. If you don't need to know it, He will not send you the word. Let's look at 1 Corinthians 13:9 again, but this time, in the NLT.

Now our knowledge is partial and incomplete, and even the gift of prophecy reveals only part of the whole picture!

You see, a prophetic word does not reveal everything in detail. In other words, a prophetic word does not reveal the process to; it only reveals the destination. It's your job to remain prayerful about the process. Think about your human relationships: your friendships, family or lover. When you share information with them, you don't normally share it just because. You divulge information because you think it's necessary or beneficial to these people in some way. Maybe, it's to teach them something, warn them about something or simply just to show them that you love them, and you are looking out for their best interest. It's the same way with God the Father. He doesn't send you a word just because He has nothing better to talk about or do. The word God sends you is to help, benefit, assist, and or warn you because He cares about you. Certainly, you will need to remember the words He said and follow His instructions to make it through or to understand whatever it is He has warned you about or is preparing you for.

A prophetic word can come in two forms. One form is what I like to call a prosperous word, which obviously is good. This is when God tells you something good. Perhaps, He will bless you with something or do something through you that will benefit you and others – something of that nature, prosperous. The other is in the form of a rebuke (which should be done in love). I guess this is also good because the word is correcting you so you can be prosperous or overcome whatever it is you need to (at least, that's the way we should view it).

Most prophetic words, in my case, were prosperous words. As I said earlier, when I first received them I was very excited. But why did the Lord send me those great, prosperous prophetic words so early in my life when He knew I wouldn't receive the manifestation of them until much later on. (Literally, as I am writing this book, I am still waiting on those prophetic words to come to pass). God did not want me to look at my life in its past and present state. He wanted me to look at what He promised me because that would be my life. To reiterate, God doesn't just send you a prophetic word because He has nothing better to do or say; He sends it because you need it.

> *Brethren, I count not myself to have apprehended: but this one thing I do, forgetting those things which are behind, and reaching forth unto those things which are before, I press toward the mark for the prize of the high calling of God in Christ Jesus.* (Philippians 3:13-14 KJV)

Sometimes, I wonder where I would be if I didn't have the promises of God to look forward to. If I had lived up to this point of my life without a promise or prophetic word from the Lord, where would I be? I can honestly say, I would feel like I have no reason to live. From experience, I've learned one interesting thing about prophecies: when it's a prosperous word, don't get too excited and caught up about the prophecy in itself thinking it will be fulfilled tomorrow. You should be more focused on learning and grasping all you need to on your journey to the prophecy or promise being fulfilled. Most times, prophetic words are so contrary to reality that in the process, you can quickly forget them, question if you heard correctly or if the prophecy was even true. Like I said earlier, God sends you a word because He knows what you need; He already knows your journey and the process you'll take to your promises. For some, the process is very challenging so the great God sends us our word of victory beforehand. He sends it before depression, doubt, and all other negative things can overtake us. We can hold on to that word and continue the sometimes difficult and draining journey.

> *So do not throw away this confident trust in the Lord. Remember the great reward it brings you! Patient endurance is what you need now, so that you will continue to do God's will. Then you will receive all that he has promised.* (Hebrews 10:35-36 NLT)

> *One night Joseph had a dream, and when he told his brothers about it, they hated him more than ever.* (Genesis 37:5 NLT)

God spoke to Joseph so many times through his dreams, and every time, God showed Joseph his life already in the prosperous state. In all of the dreams God gave Joseph, He never once showed him the pit, being sold into slavery or any of what we would consider as negative or difficult times. The Lord only showed Joseph the promises, never the process. Why is that? Well, you know the saying, "You see my glory but you don't know my story." I think that has something to do with it. There isn't anyone I know who would turn down a successful life. If God gave people the option to be rich and famous, successful beyond their wildest dreams or to just have a normal average lifestyle living from paycheck to paycheck and barely getting by, I think the majority would say, "Lord I want the successful life beyond my wildest dreams." However, I'm almost certain that if the Lord told them up front the process they would have to endure to get the prosperous, successful life beyond their wildest dreams, 99.9% of people would tell Him: "No, that's ok Lord; I'll just take a normal, average just getting by life."

Understand something about the process to your promise. It is first of all for your benefit, no matter how bad the process seems. God is neither late nor does He ever forget His promises to you no matter how long you feel He is taking to fulfill them. If you are still in the process to your promise, it's because there's still something valuable for you to learn. God is still shaping and preparing you for your promise.

> *The Lord isn't really being slow about his promise, as some people think. No, he is being patient for your sake. He does not want anyone to be destroyed, but wants everyone to repent.* (2 Peter 3:9 NLT)

Sometimes, the process may feel like it's so long that the promise will never come to pass but just look at it this way: the longer the process the greater the promise. However, no matter how long the process, there is something about a true word from the Lord that somehow always finds its way to sustain you. Don't let go of a true word from the Lord whether it is sent through a prophet, the Word of God, a dream or however the Lord chooses. At times, you may seem crazy to everyone else around you because your reality or current situation may be far from the word you received from God. It may seem impossible for the word to come to pass. Although you feel ridiculous holding on to the word, you just can't let it go. This is what I call faith.

> *Now faith is the substance of things hoped for, the evidence of things not seen.* (Hebrews 11:1 KJV)

And we all know that without faith it is impossible to please God.

> *But without faith it is impossible to please him: for he that cometh to God must believe that he is, and that he is a rewarder of them that diligently seek him.* (Hebrews 11:6 KJV)

I often think about faith on this Christian journey in general. Why do we need faith other than for the obvious reason – to please God? What does faith do for us? How does it benefit us so to speak? But how would we know we had faith if it was never tested? What would it mean if God came through right away? Would we feel like we genuinely have faith? Or would we just feel God is Santa Claus from whom we get whatever we want when we want it? When you endure and believe God for the impossible, and it becomes a reality, we know that we have faith and we truly trust God.

> *We were given this hope when we were saved. If we already have something, we don't need to hope for it. But if we look forward to something we don't yet have, we must wait patiently and confidently.* (Romans 8:24-25 NLT)

Look at it this way: God is so awesome that everything He allows us to go through is for us to come to know; whatever it is that he is teaching us through the process. God already knows everything, but as we put our faith and trust in Him, He helps us and teaches us what we need to know. It could be how much faith we have, how much we trust, believe or simply anything He wants us to know about ourselves. God is so good that He helps us to grow up to fit into our promises because if He gave them to us too early, we wouldn't handle them correctly.

> *An inheritance obtained too early in life is not a blessing in the end.* (Proverbs 20:21 NLT)

Sometimes, we want our blessings or promises from God before we are ready for them. God, being the good Father that He is, won't release anything to us that we are not ready for or can't handle. What we need to understand is that God does this to protect us because He knows what's best for us. Yes, the Bible says that God will not withhold any good thing from those who walk upright before Him.

> *For the Lord God is a sun and shield: the Lord will give grace and glory: no good thing will he withhold from them that walk uprightly.* (Psalms 84:11 KJV)

If God released the good thing to us before we are ready for it, then it won't be a good thing at all. That thing that was intended for good will very quickly become a burden, rather than a blessing if you are not equipped to handle it. The prime example of this would be a woman praying for a husband. Let's just say that this woman has a problem with submitting to men in general. And because of this, she can't see herself submitting to a husband because she has a mind of her own, and she knows how to use it.

> *As the church submits to Christ, so you wives should submit to your husbands in everything.* (Ephesians 5:24 NLT)

First of all, submitting to your husband doesn't mean you don't have a mind of your own, and you can't use it. However, most women with the mindset that they aren't going to submit to a man can't be told this because their definition of the word "submit" is control. Women, I'm sorry to tell you but if you are not ready to submit to your husband then you are not ready for your husband. Also, let's say this woman can't cook, clean, pray, and doesn't have her own personal relationship with God in order. There are some instances where the husband is a better cook than the wife so the husband does the cooking. That's fine, whatever works for the couple. However, women, don't you think you should know how to prepare a meal for your man when he comes home? Because if he can't cook himself then how do you expect God to release his king to you if you can't even feed him. God loves His son too much to let him starve (lol)! If God gave this woman that blessing in a husband, it's clear to see how easily that blessing of a husband would turn into a burden because she's simply not ready for him. Obviously, submitting to him, cooking for him, cleaning their home, and certainly keeping him covered in prayer (if she doesn't have her own personal prayer life and relationship with God) will be too much for her to handle. So why would God give her a burden?

God won't! What He'll do is shape, mold and prepare her (the process) so that when He releases her husband to her, he will be a blessing, not a burden. Women, before God can release your husbands to you the way He intended, He has to shape you into virtuous women. Otherwise, He will be releasing to you a burden, instead of a blessing; remember you are to be your husband's help mate not his hurt mate.

> *Who can find a virtuous and capable wife? She is more precious than rubies. Her husband can trust her, and she will greatly enrich his life. She brings him good, not harm, all the days of her life.* (Proverbs 31:10-12 NLT)

A woman who's not ready to be a wife who prays for a husband is just one example. The same goes for a man praying for a wife. Men, God's intended purpose for you as husbands is for you to love your wives as Christ loved the church.

> *For husbands, this means love your wives, just as Christ loved the church. He gave up his life for her.* (Ephesians 5:25 NLT)

With that being said, how can you possibly think you are ready to love a woman as your wife if you don't even know Christ to learn how He loves the church? Some of you may not even love yourselves, but you have the nerve to ask God for a wife. As a husband, you are to be the priest, prophet, and provider of your home. It's unfortunate that the closest many men today have to this is being providers; their manhood begins and ends right there. A lot of men think that they can successfully be the husbands and fathers God intended them to be without being the priests and prophets of their homes. I'm sorry to tell you brothers but until you can love your future wives the way Christ loves the church, being the priests, prophets, and providers, you are not ready to be husbands. Certainly, just loving your wife as Christ loves the church is a major responsibility in itself. However, I have news for you: that's just what being a husband is – a major RESPONSIBILITY! Therefore, how do you expect God to release that responsibility to you if you are not ready for it?

Last but not least, the same goes for employment and careers. Yes, God wants to prosper His people but we must be ready for success.

> *"For I know the plans I have for you," says the Lord. "They are plans for good and not for disaster, to give you a future and a hope."* (Jeremiah 29:11 NLT)

God is not going to just give you a job or career that you're not ready for. You may think you can handle it right now, but the truth is you may still need more training before God releases that responsibility to you.

You may very well be ready for that job or career work wise. Meaning, you are well trained and equipped for the administrative or skills workload. However, you may not exactly be ready for the people or environment that God has for you to work with and in. Not everyone is saved, sanctified, Holy Ghost filled, and fire baptized. You will work with some complicated people, to say the least. Let's not sugar coat it; some people are just outright evil. You have to know how to handle them. Therefore, on top of the preparation for the workload, God has to prepare you for the other things that come along with the job or career.

Make no mistake about it; God doesn't prepare you to change the other people's attitudes and personalities in preparing you for the job or career. What He does is change you, your attitude and perspective so that you will know how to deal with different attitudes and personalities. Prayerfully, you can influence those you work with to change them for the better.

When you are ready for the job or career, God will favor you with the right one. You will be grateful for all of the training and preparation. You will be more equipped for the task than if God had just given it to you before you were fully prepared. Another way to look at it is maybe, what you had in mind or what you were praying for is simply too small compared to what God has in mind for you. You may be praying for a particular job but God wants you to establish your own business. He may not open the door for that job because if He does, you may get too comfortable and never even think about entrepreneurship. Yes, you may be ready for the plan you have for you but are you ready for the better plan God has for you? That's why it's so important not to allow yourself to get so frustrated when things don't go your way. Rather, continue to seek God for His will and plan for your life even in the hard times. Be willing to let go of your plans for God's better plan for your life.

The last example I'll give is related to earthly parents, especially those who are well established financially. Without their children's knowledge, they have money saved up for their children – an inheritance so to speak. They may have started saving from the moment their child was conceived. Perhaps, it's for college or just to give them a head start in life when they turn 18 or 21 and are living on their own. Whatever the purpose, they wait to give the money or inheritance to their children at the appropriate time. Some even wait past the age or time they originally set if they don't feel the children have matured enough to manage it.

It's the same way with God our Father. However, unlike the earthly father, God does reveal some of His promises and our inheritance before hand through the Bible and or prophetic words. But similar to the parents, He won't release them to us until He knows that we can handle them. Remember, if God releases the good thing to us before we are ready, He will be releasing a burden, not a blessing.

I don't know about you, but I'm glad God handles us this way. Have you ever heard the saying: "I'd rather have it and don't need it than to need it and don't have it"? Well, that's the way I want my blessings to flow. Most people who weren't mature or ready for their blessings lost them because they were not prepared. They then looked back at what they had, desiring them once again; this happens way too frequently in marriages. However, when a person is disciplined, mature and waits patiently for the blessing, almost all of the time, he or she appreciates and maintains it once it's finally received. But what does all of this have to do with being mandated to live holy?

I'm sure there's something in your life that at some point made you feel different. It has a lot more to do with living holy than you think. You'll see and come to a better understanding of your life's situations when you continue reading. But first, let's talk about a mandate and what it means. A mandate is an official order or commission to do something; it's basically a must. What is holy? One definition of the word "holy" is being dedicated or consecrated to God for a religious purpose, sacred. Therefore, Mandated to live Holy is a "must" to live for God. I pray this book will bring you to the understanding that although the choice is yours, it is a "must" for you to live for God – MANDATED TO LIVE HOLY.

Chapter 2

KNOWING WHO WE REALLY ARE

Satan's task is to keep you from knowing who you are.

When we understand the importance of the mandate for us to live holy, it's easy to comprehend why it's so important for Satan, the Enemy, to keep us from it. His most prized possession in doing so is to prevent us from knowing who we really are.

Before I formed you in the womb I knew you, before you were born I set you apart; I appointed you as a prophet to the nations. (Jeremiah 1:5 NIV)

God created Jeremiah to be a prophet to the nations; that was specifically who He called Jeremiah to be. I can't tell you who God has called you to be. Only God knows that. It's your job to seek Him about it. As with Jeremiah, God the Father had already formed you, set you apart, and appointed you for all that you are to be even before you were conceived in your mother's womb. For clarity, an example would be a tree of any kind, grown to its full potential, which was always meant to grow into that fully grown tree from the start. However, it was not planted in the ground when it was fully grown. Rather, it was planted as a little seed and as time went on, with proper care, it grew to its full potential. It became the big, strong, beautiful tree that it was always meant to be.

That's similar to what God is saying to us in this scripture. Before He formed us in the womb, He already knew the overall big plan He had in mind for our purpose and destiny. However, we develop into that masterpiece day by day with proper care, discipline, and patience. It's during this development that the Enemy tries to keep us from discovering and growing into God's overall big plan.

Satan is a liar; that's a truth we should understand. Therefore, he's against the truth. It's no surprise that he would work so hard to keep us from knowing the truth about who God is and who we are in God. As long as Satan is successful in keeping us ignorant in this first area he doesn't even have to worry about deceiving us in any other areas. If he can keep us from knowing whose and who we are, he's pretty much got us where he wants us. He will keep us from going where God wants us to go and from being who God created us to be.

Although we are all individuals with no two of us being exactly alike (not even identical twins), we all possess one similarity. It's the first thing that Satan tries to keep us from acknowledging –where we all came from. All of us were created by God the Father. Therefore, we are all God's creation. Nevertheless, although we are created in His image (to think for ourselves and make our own decisions), God does not force Himself on us. I heard it said so many times that God is a gentleman. We were all created by God the Father; we had no say in the matter. However, we have to choose whether or not we want to follow Him and be called His children; that choice is ours. God will not force us to follow Him.

> *Today I have given you the choice between life and death, between blessings and curses. Now I call on heaven and earth to witness the choice you make. Oh, that you would choose life, so that you and your descendants might live!* (Deuteronomy 30:19 NLT)

What is a child of God? How do I know if I am a child of God or not? The answer to that is to first receive Jesus Christ, God's Son as your Lord and Savior.

> *For you are all children of God through faith in Christ Jesus.* (Galatians 3:26 NLT)

Chapter 2 • Knowing Who We Really Are

> *Jesus told him, "I am the way, the truth, and the life. No one can come to the Father except through me.* (John 14:6 NLT)

> *Anyone who denies the Son doesn't have the Father, either. But anyone who acknowledges the Son has the Father also.* (1 John 2:23 NLT)

Once you've received Jesus Christ as your Lord and Savior, there are some characteristics as a child of God that you should possess.

> *Those who have been born into God's family do not make a practice of sinning, because God's life is in them. So they can't keep on sinning, because they are children of God. So now we can tell who are children of God and who are children of the devil. Anyone who does not live righteously and does not love other believers does not belong to God.* (1 John 3:9-10 NLT)

> *Since we know that Christ is righteous, we also know that all who do what is right are God's children.* (1 John 2:29 NLT)

> *For all who are lead by the spirit of God are children of God.* (Romans 8:14 NLT)

Galatians 5:22-23 NLT gives a clear description of the characteristics of a child of God, it states "But the fruit of the Spirit is love, joy, peace, longsuffering, gentleness, goodness, faith, meekness, temperance: against such there is no law."

Why are these scriptures requirements to be a child of God? Because just as children in the natural reflect their parents in some way, we need to do the same with God our Father. Not all children look like their parents; however, almost all of the time, there's something about their characters that are reflections of the parents. If a child doesn't physically look like their parents, he or she may have mannerisms, attitudes, body gestures or something about them to identify them with the parents. The same ought to be for us as children of God.

Let's look at a family in the natural to better help you understand our free choice to accept God as our Father and be called His child or not. We will use a nuclear family consisting of a father, mother, and four children, for example. All four children were conceived by the same parents; they have the same blood running through their veins. Yet, all of the children are different and all may choose different lifestyles. Let's say three of the four children choose the lifestyle their parents raised them to have but one didn't because that particular child felt the lifestyle he or she wanted to pursue was better.

The child's choice of lifestyle, which is different from his or her parents does not take away the fact that he or she is their child. However, if that child decides to separate from the parents because of the choice of lifestyle, he or she chooses to be distant from the family members and lose. By distancing themselves children risk losing the benefits of discovering who they are as well as; receiving other significant help from their parents. For example, children who decide to live on their own because they disagree with the lifestyle the parents want for them are no longer the responsibility of the parents. By moving out, they have removed themselves from the parents' covering, which includes shelter, food, clothing, spending money, and guidance because they have chosen a different direction (lifestyle) in life.

God created all of us. He is the Father of all creation; nothing and no one can take that away. Just like the child in the example, we have no say in who our parents are (no one has any say in God being the Father of all creation): "Yet, O Lord, you are our Father. We are the clay, and you are the potter. We all are formed by your hand" (Isaiah 64: 8 NLT). The child in this example has free will to accept or reject his parents' teachings, love, protection, provision, and guidance and to apply it to his or her life (reflecting that he is their child). Likewise, we can accept or reject our Father's teachings, love, protection, provision, and guidance and apply it to our lives to reflect that we are God's children.

The Enemy at some point in our lives whether we grew up believing in God or not works very hard daily to get us far away from God. His intention is to make us forget God even created us, we came from Him, and we belong to Him, not ourselves.

> *The earth is the Lord's, and the fullness thereof; the world, and they that dwell therein.* (Psalms 24:1 KJV)

We all belong to God the Father. But at some point in our lives whether knowingly or unknowingly, we reject God the same way earthly children reject their parents. We go out on our own to discover lives that God the Father tried to save us from, to begin with. But there is a difference between children who accept their parents' values and principles and the children who do not. In the example, the children who stayed home, obeyed, and learned from their parents' teachings benefitted because they had direct access to their parents for whatever they needed. If they had a question, didn't understand something, were facing challenges or just simply needed their parents to get something for them, they were at an advantage. Why? They were in their parents' presence. Furthermore, they were being protected and prepared by their parents for what they were unaware of, which is what most parents like to call – the real world.

On the other hand, the children outside the parents' presence (their home) did not have these privileges. Even worse, they may settle for the counterfeit of the things they need from people who are insincere and can't be trusted; people who don't genuinely want to help them. They only use them to get what they really want. It's unlike the unconditional love that their earthly parents and God the Father have for them. By the way, this is exactly what the Enemy does. He deceives us causing us to leave the truth to follow and believe lies.

We all have one thing in common; we all come from God the Father. However, we choose either to stay with God and live out His intended purpose for our lives or to go our own routes leaving Him, His principles, ways, and benefits. By our lifestyles we choose whether or not we want to be called God's children. If we want to live lifestyles contrary to the one God the Father has for us then we disown God as our Father and leave His protection and benefits.

As I said earlier, not everyone was born and raised in the church or a home where God was acknowledged. Some were born and raised in homes where God wasn't discussed. Some people have parents who are atheists and others come from homes of Satan worshipers. But God is so loving He will still find a way to reach you and give you a chance to make the choice to receive him. Will you accept or reject His Son Jesus Christ? Will you serve God and be called His child?

God created all of us for His purpose and glory. However, there are some who reject God and choose to live in darkness. Choosing a life of darkness is what happens when the Enemy is successful in keeping us from knowing to whom we really belong. When this happens, we believe we belong to ourselves and some people in ignorance have even given themselves over to Satan (those who partake in witchcraft and things of that nature). Now as I said, there are cases where people truly just don't know God or of Him. Maybe, they weren't raised in a Christian home. Maybe, up to a certain point, they have never even heard of God (Jesus Christ). However, as I said, I don't believe that God doesn't give them a chance to know the truth about who He is. If that's you and you're reading this book, now is your chance to receive the truth (Jesus Christ). The reality is if you choose to believe the lie from the Enemy and reject God our Father, you have chosen a life of darkness and basically have turned yourself over to the Enemy.

> *Since they thought it foolish to acknowledge God, he abandoned them to their foolish thinking and let them do things that should never be done. Their lives became full of every kind of wickedness, sin, greed, hate, envy, murder, quarreling, deception, malicious behavior, and gossip. They are backstabbers, haters of God, insolent, proud, and boastful. They invent new ways of sinning, and they disobey their parents. They refuse to understand, break their promises, are heartless, and have no mercy. They know God's justice requires that those who do these things deserve to die, yet they do them anyway. Worse yet, they encourage others to do them, too.* (Romans 1:28-32 NLT)

Some people ask: "If God is real, and He is such a loving God then how can He allow such evil to take place in life? Why do murders, rape, robberies, and all types of crimes and hurtful things occur?" Of course, I'm not God so I don't have the answer to these questions but, could the above scripture be the answer? Could it be that people's willingness to reject God and welcome evil in their lives bring upon all, the evil in this world? Just a little something to think about!

I can hear someone saying: "Well, I never knew I had 'rules' to follow to be called a child of God." First of all, let me encourage you to try not to view it as rules but as standards. With that being said, maybe, you did know about these standards but up until this point of your life, it's been too difficult to follow all of them. Perhaps, you've done so many things contrary to the characteristics of a child of God that you've just accepted the lie that you're not good enough to be a child of God. I want you to understand that it doesn't matter what you've done in life. Nothing you've done will ever disqualify you from God's love and being His child if you repent and turn to Him.

The other important thing I want you to know is that viewing God's standards as "rules" may be keeping you from carrying them out. When we think about laws and the consequences of disobeying them, it's understandable how we can view the standards of being a child of God as obeying "rules." There are some similarities; however, there are also differences. If most people had the choice to disobey the law and get away with it, they probably would. But when you are a child of God and have fallen in love with Him, even if God gave you a free pass to disobey Him, you wouldn't want to.

Once you have an intimate relationship with God, these standards, which some may call "rules" are not viewed as such. They become a part of you, a part of your nature. You desire to be like God and, of course, to please Him. You will come to a place where you desire to follow this way of living because whether you realize it or not, you are allowing God to live through you. If these standards do feel like a set of rules to you right now, don't beat yourself up. It will feel this way if you are new to this. As a matter of fact, it's supposed to feel this way. But much like with anything else, with time, it will be your true nature as the child of God that you are. It is important to understand that when God tells us not to do something, it's to protect us from something. When He tells us to do something, it's to direct us to something. Whether or not you understand God's standards, try to remember that God who has infinite knowledge gives His instructions for a reason. Although what

He says may make little or no sense to you at the time, it is for your ultimate benefit.

> *All Scripture is inspired by God and is useful to teach us what is true and to make us realize what is wrong in our lives. It corrects us when we are wrong and teaches us to do what is right. God uses it to prepare and equip his people to do every good work.* (2 Timothy 3:16-17 NLT)

So you see, the standards God has set for His children in the Bible are to teach us what we are to be like. Therefore, rather than seeing them as chores, obligations or a set of rules as I said in the beginning, look at them as your training ground or boot camp. When a person is in either of these achieving the goal appears to be very difficult and sometimes, seems very distant during the training process. There may even be some days when it feels impossible to accomplish the objective and as if they'll never learn how to get the job done. However, after much practice day by day, eventually, the person not only "gets it" but he or she masters it so well that it looks easy to those on the outside looking in. It's the same with following these standards as a child of God. Though they may be difficult to follow in the beginning, with the help of the Holy Spirit and daily practice, you will eventually master them. It will no longer feel like a duty but more like an honor.

> *God decided in advance to adopt us into his own family by bringing us to himself through Jesus Christ. This is what he wanted to do, and it gave him great pleasure.* (Ephesians 1:5 NLT)

The most important thing from this scripture that I want you to get is that God decided in advance to love us! He's God; therefore, He knows everything. So when He decided in advance to love us, He already knew who He was choosing to love. That means nothing we do can keep us from God's love if we repent from our sins. God is ready and faithful to forgive us.

> *No power in the sky above or in the earth below—indeed, nothing in all creation will ever be able to separate us from the love of God that is revealed in Christ Jesus our Lord.* (Romans 8:39 NLT)

The Enemy's whole purpose is to trick you out of believing in God's love for you. He also wants to prevent you from believing and receiving God as your Father and from being God's child. The Enemy may trick you out of this in several ways. If you haven't been brought up in church or you've never heard of Jesus, he will try to keep you from hearing of or paying attention to what you hear from God. He will also lead or attempt to lead you into so many things that are contrary to God. In doing so, when you do hear of or pay attention to God and His ways, you'll feel unworthy or incapable of receiving Him and His love.

The Enemy also tries to trick you and keep you from coming to God by deceiving you into believing there is no God. He also encourages you to persecute God and believers of God because of your unbelief. But what may surprise you is that not even your passion for persecuting God can keep you from His love for you. Believe it or not, even your persecution of God is a part of your journey to lead you straight to God. If that's you, my brother or sister, you are in great company. Have you ever heard of a man in the Bible named Saul? Or maybe, you know him as Paul. Well, he became one of God's most powerful apostles but before that, he was a persecutor of God's people.

> *Meanwhile, Saul was uttering threats with every breath and was eager to kill the Lord's followers. So he went to the high priest. He requested letters addressed to the synagogues in Damascus, asking for their cooperation in the arrest of any followers of the Way he found there. He wanted to bring them—both men and women—back to Jerusalem in chains. As he was approaching Damascus on this mission, a light from heaven suddenly shone down around him. He fell to the ground and heard a voice saying to him, "Saul! Saul! Why are you persecuting me?" "Who are you, lord?" Saul asked. And the voice replied, "I am Jesus, the one you are persecuting! Now get up and go into the city, and you will be told what you must do." The men with Saul stood speechless, for they heard the sound of someone's voice but saw no one! Saul picked himself up off the ground, but when he opened his eyes he was blind. So his companions led him by the hand to Damascus. He remained there blind for three days and did not eat or drink. Now there was a believer in Damascus named Ananias. The Lord spoke to*

> *him in a vision, calling, "Ananias!" "Yes, Lord!" he replied. The Lord said, "Go over to Straight Street, to the house of Judas. When you get there, ask for a man from Tarsus named Saul. He is praying to me right now. I have shown him a vision of a man named Ananias coming in and laying hands on him so he can see again." "But Lord," exclaimed Ananias, "I've heard many people talk about the terrible things this man has done to the believers in Jerusalem! And he is authorized by the leading priests to arrest everyone who calls upon your name." But the Lord said, "Go, for Saul is my chosen instrument to take my message to the Gentiles and to kings, as well as to the people of Israel. And I will show him how much he must suffer for my name's sake." So Ananias went and found Saul. He laid his hands on him and said, "Brother Saul, the Lord Jesus, who appeared to you on the road, has sent me so that you might regain your sight and be filled with the Holy Spirit." Instantly something like scales fell from Saul's eyes, and he regained his sight. Then he got up and was baptized.* (Act 9:1-18 NLT)

If you are like Saul who persecuted the believers of Christ or engaged in a lifestyle that you thought disqualified you from being a child of God, intentionally or unintentionally, I've got good news for you. God the Father is waiting for you to simply recognize your sin and repent. Acknowledge God and repent of your sins; He'll put you in right standing with Him. I decree and declare right now, in the name of Jesus that as you do so just as with Saul, the scales will fall from your eyes, and you will see the truth clearly.

> *Repent, then, and turn to God, so that your sins may be wiped out, that times of refreshing may come from the Lord.* (Acts 3:19 NIV)

If you've never accepted Jesus Christ the Son of God as your Lord and Savior, now would be a good time for that as well. Need some help? Repeat this prayer to God the Father:

> *Father God, in the name of Jesus, I acknowledge my sins (voice them) before You right now. I'm sorry for the wrongs I've done; I have indulged in this lifestyle contrary to the life You have for me to live. Forgive me, Father, and help me to forgive myself. God, I believe You are my father; I believe in Your Son Jesus Christ. I may not understand why, but I believe that He died*

for my sins, and You raised Him from the dead. I accept Jesus Christ into my heart right now as my Lord and Savior. Father, give me the strength and power to conquer temptations and help me to always remember that I am Your child but my sins keep me separated from You. I never want to be separated from You again. You are my Father, and I am Your child. I need You now and forever. In Jesus' name, I pray. Amen.

If you said that prayer from your heart (and trust me God knows your heart) then congratulations!!! You are saved, forgiven, and on your way to living your life as God intended you to – as the child of God that you are!

If you openly declare that Jesus is Lord and believe in your heart that God raised him from the dead, you will be saved. For it is by believing in your heart that you are made right with God, and it is by openly declaring your faith that you are saved. (Romans 10:9-10 NLT)

Congratulations! You've just declared it. You are God's and God is yours. You are a child of the King of kings. Now that you're aware of this, I'm sure you want to know why the Enemy works first on keeping you from knowing whose you are. He does it because once you know whose you are then you come to know who you are. It's just like in the natural where an important part of knowing who you are includes knowing your family history, your race, culture, where you come from and things of that nature. Well, we all know that there is no race with God because God is a spirit.

For God is Spirit, so those who worship him must worship in spirit and in truth. (John 4:24 NLT)

Therefore, knowing God and your family line through Him is knowing the character of God, the authority and power of God, the promises of God, and all of the attributes of God.

And since we are his children, we are his heirs. In fact, together with Christ we are heirs of God's glory. But if we are to share his glory, we must also share his suffering. (Romans 8:17 NLT)

As in any royal family, the king leaves an inheritance for his children and family. And of course, they have many benefits while he is alive. Therefore, when you know who God is, what He possesses and what He has given His children, you understand your worth, power, and authority as well. Knowing whose we are and the power He has given us, leads us to operate in who we are. But the Enemy consistently and defiantly tries to keep us from doing so. As children of God who are we? We are more than conquerors, which means we have power over the Enemy and over everything that comes our way.

> *Behold, I give unto you power to tread on serpents and scorpions, and over all the power of the enemy: and nothing shall by any means hurt you.* (Luke 10:19 KJV)

As a child of God, you have great power and authority. Do you see now why it's so important for the Enemy to keep you from knowing this? When we know and operate in who we really are, the Enemy, the one who comes to steal, kill, and destroy is fearful. He doesn't want us to know who we are because he doesn't want us to destroy him. What does he do? He disguises himself when he's at work to keep us off track so that we won't recognize and destroy him. He does this by keeping us distracted from the truth and what matters. He keeps us focused on the lies he presents to us to shift us away from being who we really are – children of God. What is the truth? The truth is:

> *For we wrestle not against flesh and blood, but against principalities, against powers, against the rulers of the darkness of this world, against spiritual wickedness in high places.* (Ephesians 6:12 KJV)

The Enemy is crafty and cunning. He deceives us into thinking that we are each other's enemies. As a result, we kill and destroy one another when in fact, we should be fighting against him – the real Enemy. The Devil uses many strategies to trick and confuse us, but two of the most powerful are jealousy and envy. We become so jealous and envious of each other that we are consumed by hatred, which in turn prevents us from exercising our gifts and talents. We hate the singer so much that

God can't show us the songwriter in us. We become so jealous of the one whom the Lord just blessed with a house that God can't show us the gift of carpentry He has given us to build houses; the list goes on and on. We get so distracted by hatred and our desire for each other's gifts and blessings that God can't show us the gifts and talents He has placed in us for His glory. Moreover, we cannot see the blessings God has for us because we are so focused on what He has blessed others with. We desire their blessings instead of the ones God has with our very name on them.

One thing I've learned about human beings is that we are the most unsatisfied creation. We seem to be content with what we have; we even love what we have until we see what someone else has. We like our hair; we think it's the perfect length, texture, and everything else until we see someone else's hair. We like our figure; we even look in the mirror and say to ourselves: "Man if I was the opposite sex I would die for me" until we see someone else's figure. We like our cars; we wash them daily and even cried when we got them, full of gratitude until we see our neighbor's. We like our spouses and think they're the best thing that ever happened to us until – uh, oh – let me stop there (lol).

Remember Lucifer, with all that he had and all that he was in heaven, he still was not satisfied. Instead, he wanted to be God. Consequently, God took all of what he had away from him and kicked him out of heaven

> *How art thou fallen from heaven, O Lucifer, son of the morning! How art thou cut down to the ground, which didst weaken the nations! For thou hast said in thine heart, I will ascend into heaven, I will exalt my throne above the stars of God: I will sit also upon the mount of the congregation, in the sides of the north: I will ascend above the heights of the clouds; I will be like the most high. Yet thou shalt be brought down to hell, to the sides of the pit.* (Isaiah 14:12-15 KJV)

What we should learn from Satan's fall is to be content and grateful for how God has made us, what He has made us for, and the way He blesses and uses us individually. We need to always remember that God created us to be different for a reason. He gave us different gifts and talents and blesses us in a variety of ways for His glory, to build His kingdom and edify the saints; this is crucial to remember. When we allow the Enemy to trick us into being jealous of our sisters' or brothers' gifts, we lose focus and sometimes, never even come into the knowledge of our own gifts. One danger in this is that because the Enemy is a liar, he will not only make us hate our brothers or sisters for their gifts, he will lie to us and make us believe that we have that same gift, and we can operate in it even better than them. God help us all when the catastrophe of the manifestation of this takes place.

I'm sure we've all had the experience of seeing someone attempt to operate in a gift that was not his or hers. I've experienced it many times but the best illustration I can give is a person who does not possess the gift of singing but attempts to function in that gift. Shows like American Idol (the auditions) have allowed us to experience this horror. Just think of how terrible that non-singer's selection sounded in your ears. Well, that's how harmful we are to the body of Christ when we try to operate in someone else's gift, instead of the one God has given us. Our service to God sounds just as bad to Him as that non-singer's selection did to us when we try to operate in someone else's gift out of jealousy or better yet, not operating in any gift from our hearts. It's so important to find your gift and operate in it, not someone else's. All gifts and talents are needed in the body of Christ, but everyone must operate in his or her own gift and talent in order for them to work together effectively for the upliftment of God's kingdom and the edifying of the saints.

That's right; we are not only to build up the kingdom of God but also edify each other.

> *A spiritual gift is given to each of us so we can help each other. To one person the Spirit gives the ability to give wise advice to another the same Spirit gives a message of special knowledge. The same Spirit gives great faith to another, and to someone else the one Spirit gives the gift of healing. He gives one person the power to perform miracles, and another the ability to prophesy. He gives someone else the ability to discern whether a message is from the Spirit of God or from another spirit. Still another person is given*

Chapter 2 • Knowing Who We Really Are

the ability to speak in unknown languages, while another is given the ability to interpret what is being said. It is the one and only Spirit who distributes all these gifts. He alone decides which gift each person should have. The human body has many parts, but the many parts make up one whole body. So it is with the body of Christ. (1 Corinthians 12:7-12 NLT)

But our bodies have many parts, and God has put each part just where he wants it. How strange a body would be if it had only one part! Yes, there are many parts, but only one body. The eye can never say to the hand, "I don't need you." The head can't say to the feet, "I don't need you." (1 Corinthians 12:18-21 NLT)

We are all needed in the body of Christ and so are our gifts. So how can we edify each other if we're busy hating one another and tearing each other down? We can't! We only destroy each other this way and guess what? We take on the character of the Devil and assist him in tearing down God's kingdom. It's important to know our gifts and to operate in them, but doing so is only half the battle. The main focus we need to have isn't on our gifts or talents; it's on who we are. Our gifts and talents help us present who we are but who we are is what the Enemy tries to keeps us from knowing and operating in. So who are we? We are God's children.

Being the children of God, we are made in the image and likeness of God. We have been given the power and authority to rule and govern this world:

Then God said, "let us make human beings in our image, to be like us. They will reign over the fish in the sea, the birds in the sky, the livestock, all the wild animals on the earth, and the small animals that scurry along the ground." So God created human beings in his own image. In the image of God he created them; male and female he created them. Then God blessed them and said, "Be fruitful and multiply. Fill the earth and govern it. Reign over the fish in the sea, the birds in the sky, and all the animals that scurry along the ground." (Genesis 1:26-28 NLT)

What does this mean to you? What is the image of God to you? Do you realize that how you view God is how you should view yourself because you are made in His image and likeness? Therefore, should you view yourself as worthless? Maybe, you don't view God as worthy; should you view yourself as poor? Maybe, you don't view God as rich, the owner of a thousand cattle on a hill. If you view yourself as powerless, then you don't view God as all-powerful. You don't recognize He has given you the power and authority through His Holy Spirit to overcome every situation that comes your way. What does all of this mean? You have the power and authority over your problems and situations! You have the power and authority over the Enemy! I know some of you disagree with me on this, and that's just what the Enemy wants you to do and how he wants you to feel but thank God, I have a witness. Again, I say:

> *Behold, I give unto you power to tread on serpents and scorpions, and over all the power of the enemy; and nothing shall by any means hurt you.* (Luke 10:19 KJV)

As said before, the Enemy doesn't want you to know who you are and the power you possess. He doesn't want you to expose or destroy him. That's why his first and most important task is to keep you from discovering whose and who you are. But thank God, if you have gotten this far in this book, you have now been informed of whose and who you really are. And if you dare to believe, receive, and act on it, the Enemy will shake in his tracks. However, that, of course, doesn't mean he'll back away and leave you to be who God has made and called you to be. Oh, no. Now, and I mean right now, he's working on tricking you out of everything you just read about who God and you really are.

Satan's Task to Trick You out of Believing Who You Are

You are made in the image and likeness of God; you are God's child. Therefore, you have inherited the power and authority of God to destroy the Enemy. Maybe, this is the first time you are hearing this or perhaps, you've heard it before but after reading this you actually understand and believe it. If that is so, be aware that the Enemy will do everything in his power to trick you out of believing it. How will he do this? By doing what he does best; lying, attacking, and distracting you in every way possible throughout your life.

Notice the title here: "Satan's Task to Trick You out of Believing Who You Are." Not Satan's task to trick you out of KNOWING who you are. Believing and knowing are two different things. We know with our intellects; we believe with our hearts. Some of the things that cause us to know are facts, evidence, things that we can see. What causes us to believe is faith, which is the substance of things hoped for and the evidence of things not seen. In the previous chapters, you were given lots of information about whose and who you are supported by scripture to help you understand and embrace that truth. However, to actually live out whose and who you are, you have to believe it!

> *And so it happened just as the Scriptures say: "Abraham believed God, and God counted him as righteous because of his faith." He was even called the friend of God.* (James 2:23 NLT)

I believe this is why our faith is tested. Forget about the enemy. Sometimes, we need to prove to ourselves what we believe. It's easy to believe or say we believe in something that is tangible or visible because it is evident. But that is knowing, not believing. Because God is a spirit, we cannot see or touch Him. Thus, the Enemy uses this as his main argument to deceive us into believing that God is not real or He is not present. His deceit keeps many from believing God and believing in God.

Of course, if the Enemy can keep us from believing in God, certainly, he would have no problem making us believe we are not God's children with power and authority. The Enemy's tactics keep people focused on what they can see in the natural, instead of what they know in the spirit.

> *For in this hope we were saved. But hope that is seen is no hope at all. Who hopes for what he already has? But if we hope for what we do not yet have, we wait for it patiently.* (Romans 8:24-25 NIV)

He keeps unbelievers from believing in God and similarly, he will keep us from believing who we are in God. He'll say to the unbeliever: "How can you believe in a God you can't see?" And he'll say to the believer: "How can you believe in a 'you' that you don't see?" It's the "you" that God already created you to be, but you have to grow into it. This works on unbelievers. How? The Enemy presents them with a god they can see as well as the "them" they can see. What's the god that they can see? Idols (Buddha, statues) money, status, friends, and all sorts of other priorities and physical presentations; these are things that in most instances can be controlled and produced. The Enemy causes us to make things we can control and produce our gods; isn't that something? He does the same thing with us in keeping us from believing who we really are.

He does this by causing us to focus on our problems, circumstances, and all of the things with physical or emotional evidence. Instead of affirming what God says: "'For I know the plans I have for you,' says the Lord. 'They are plans for good and not for disaster, to give you a future and a hope'" (Jeremiah 29:11 NLT). What does that tell us? The Enemy keeps us from believing who we really are through our thoughts.

For as he thinks within himself, so he is. (Proverbs 23:7 NASB)

But how do we think about something that is not when all we see is what is. All we see are our problems, circumstances, poverty, abandonment, the abuse and fear of it, our insecurities and flaws. Are these negatives the only things that exist? Or are they the only things you're looking at? In other words, we tend to think most about what we focus on most. If we focus on the negative, then that's what we tend to think about. I'm not saying we should ignore our problems. As a matter of fact, to do so may create more problems. What I'm saying is that we need to change our focus from the problem to the problem solver. He will lead us to the solutions.

Be mindful that the Enemy who comes to steal, kill, and destroy wants the worst for you; God the Father wants the best for you. Therefore, it's the Enemy's job to make you focus on the negative, but also to keep you from even seeing the positive. He wants you to be engrossed by the negative and stay down whereas God wants you to see the positive and come up. It's the Enemy who wants you to have and keep a negative perspective on things to cease your progress. But God wants you to have a positive perspective, even in the negative situations to keep you uplifted.

Have you ever thought that maybe, your life was set up the way it was on purpose? For example, have you ever worked hard for something and watched someone who didn't work for it at all get it? I'm sure we all have. Why is that? Because our lives are set. For everything we go through, God has a reason and a purpose. So could it be that your circumstances are there to teach and train you for the already intensive purpose God has for you? Does God want to shape and mold you into exactly who He created you to be? Why not pay more attention to finding solutions, rather than focusing on the problems. Is it possible that you went through the hurt so you could experience God's love? Were you betrayed to understand that God is trustworthy? Is it possible you faced abandonment to accept that God is always with you?

Would there be AA meetings to help people overcome alcoholism if no one ever abused then overcame alcohol? Would there ever be schools to teach if no one was ever taught? What we go through in life is not to punish us and make our lives miserable. It's for us to learn and grow so we can turn around and help somebody else who is going through the same thing.

> *He comforts us in all our troubles so that we can comfort others. When they are troubled, we will be able to give them the same comfort God has given us.* (2 Corinthians 1:4 NLT)

Who would listen to a teacher who hadn't studied or practiced his or her craft to teach what he or she was teaching? Or who would pay an unhealthy, overweight and out of shape personal trainer to train them? No one! The point is we must go through what we have to go through to be authentic and genuinely help others. I believe that's God's purpose for our life experiences. But the Enemy lies and tells us that a loving God would not allow us to go through such afflictions and trials.

Have you ever watched how eagles teach their young ones? In teaching their baby's how to soar, they take them to the highest mountain, all the way to the top and drop them until they open their wings and learn how to fly. Now, do you think that the birds and eagles do this because they don't love their babies and want to see them fall and die? Of course not! They do it because they love them, and they're preparing them for life and survival. So it is with God the Father.

As children of God, there are certain things that we can ask God for. Being the good Father that He is, He will give them to us. However, if He did this every time we asked for something what would we learn? More importantly, what part of God's will for our lives would we be preventing from happening? Jesus, our great example understood this:

> *Don't you realize that I could ask my Father for thousands of angels to protect us, and he would send them instantly? But if I did, how would the Scriptures be fulfilled that describe what must happen now?* (Matthew 26:53-54 NLT)

It's funny how we think that the perfect life would be one where every day is sunshine, and we don't have any challenges; we just live happily ever after. But if that was so, don't you think that life would be a little useless and boring? The excitement about life is experimenting, learning, and growing each day. Nothing teaches you better than life itself, which sometimes, consist of difficult seasons. However, if we face those difficult times with a positive perspective the way God intends for us to, we will learn what we're supposed to learn and enjoy the fullness of life even through the trials.

> *I have told you all this so that you may have peace in me. Here on earth you will have many trials and sorrows. But take heart, because I have overcome the world."* (John 16:33 NLT)

The important thing is for us to endure and overcome the hard times we face, not to stay there and be defeated. This is why we have to control our thinking, and not allow the Enemy to. An easy way to do this is to remember that the Enemy wants us to focus on the negative in any and every situation, but God wants us to find and focus on the positive. I'll tell you a secret: when you carefully examine your life with the challenges you've faced, the problems you've been through, the purpose of it and the solutions to it, you'll find a great part of your overall purpose in life in general, and the keys to your destiny. Remember, the Enemy wants to keep you from believing who you really are by invading your thoughts to keep you focused on your current or past negative circumstances. But God wants to shape and mold you into who you really are. He wants to execute that great big plan He had in mind for you when He created you. But you have to believe what God says over what the Enemy says about you for God's plan to override the Enemy's. Furthermore, you must guard your mind.

Chapter 3

....

GUARDING YOUR MIND

To help you understand the importance of guarding your mind, allow me to first share with you some reasons why the Enemy attacks your mind. He wants to keep you unfocused, distracted, and disconnected from the truth. Everything the Enemy places in your mind is intended to steer you away from knowing the truth. His aim is to lead you to believe the lies he's telling you. The Enemy's sole purpose in attacking your mind is to keep you in a carnal mindset and away from using your Christ-mind by which you think like Christ and fulfill God's purpose for your life. In doing so, God's glory is revealed through you to the earth.

It's no secret that there's no action that is performed without the thought of it first entering the mind. All actions both good and bad, everything we do, create, and desire begin as thoughts in our minds before they are brought to reality. What does that tell us? It tells me that my mind is one of the most important parts of my body to guard. What good is a person's body if he or she is brain dead? If a person is brain dead, though the rest of his or her body parts may be in good condition, they can't function because the brain isn't alive to tell them what to do. That's just it. Our brains dictate what we do. That's why the Enemy wants to control our minds. He wants to get us to do what he wants us to do and to keep us away from doing what God wants us to do.

I think it's safe to say that almost everyone does what makes sense to them. It may not make much sense to everyone else but if it makes sense to the individual, then more than likely that's what he or she is going to do. Here's one thing I've found to be true: because we are living in this world and see and experience all that we do, we can't control everything that enters our minds. Evil thoughts, negative thoughts, depressing thoughts, and all other kinds of thoughts will enter our minds because of all that we're exposed to. I don't believe we have control over that. In other words, sometimes, we don't have control over what we see and experience from day to day. However, what we do have control over is our perspectives, the thoughts that enter our minds and what we will do with them.

What makes up our perspectives or mentality? There are several factors including our upbringing, the way we are raised, and the most common, our life experiences. What's the problem associated with our perspectives or mentality being developed by our upbringing and life experiences? These things aren't always positive. Therefore, they don't always bring about positive perspectives or mentalities in life. What I'm saying is it may be naturally easier for a person with positive life experiences to guard his or her mind (guarding it to keep it thinking positive). But what about the person who encountered negative life experiences? Chances are, he or she will have a negative perspective and mentality about life. How is that individual supposed to guard his or her mind? Well, we've already established that we are children of God. Therefore, we need to follow His instructions in life, not the instructions of this world, which advocate an eye for an eye and a tooth for a tooth. Basically, if someone does you wrong, you take revenge and render evil for evil. Sometimes, you do greater harm to the person than was done to you. But how do we follow God's instructions in a world that dictates the opposite of what He says? Scripture says:

> *Throw off your old sinful nature and your former way of life, which is corrupted by lust and deception. Instead, let the Spirit renew your thoughts and attitudes.* (Ephesians 4:22-23 NLT)

This means that your life experiences, upbringing, the most common thoughts or the thoughts that make the most sense to you are not the thoughts that God wants you to be led by. Because those thoughts whether you realize it or not were corrupted by lust and deception. God says to let the Spirit renew your thoughts and attitudes. Make no mistake about it; this will take some discipline because this is not the natural way of thinking. Instead, it's allowing the Holy Spirit to think through you. It's basically saying to yourself, "Yes this or that makes the most sense to me in this situation. I think if I do this it would be best but what would Jesus do?"

I know it sounds cliché, but that is the best way to manage your thinking especially as you begin the process of letting the Holy Spirit renew your mind and attitude. When your brain can't think anything positive or can't seem to resist carnal thoughts, ask yourself no matter what the situation: "What would Jesus do?" It will help you overcome carnal thoughts and focus on the spiritual thoughts, which God wants you to think about. Some of you may be saying, "Yeah, that sounds good and all, but it's not realistic." I'll say to you: "Right, letting the Spirit renew your thoughts is not realistic, thinking carnally is." However, as children of God, we are not called to think realistically; we are called to think and be spiritual. We are Christians; therefore, we are to be Christlike.

What was Christ like? Did His thinking and treatment of people always make Him look meek, mild, and soft? Was He a coward just letting people treat Him any kind of way because He was the saved, sanctified, nice, Christian guy? Absolutely not! Jesus was gangster ya'll (lol)! But seriously, Jesus was kind, yet, stern when necessary and He was also intelligent. Jesus avoided most confrontations with His intelligence. He never had to fist fight because He always beat or outsmarted His opponents with His brilliance or should I say, with the Word of God.

One day as Jesus was teaching the people and preaching the Good News in the Temple, the leading priests, the teachers of religious law, and the elders came up to him. They demanded, "By what authority are you doing all these things? Who gave you the right?" "Let me ask you a question first," he replied. "Did John's authority to baptize come from heaven, or was it merely human?"

They talked it over among themselves. "If we say it was from heaven, he will ask why we didn't believe John. But if we say it was merely human, the people will stone us because they are convinced John was a prophet." So they finally replied that they didn't know. And Jesus responded, "Then I won't tell you by what authority I do these things." (Luke 20:1-8 NLT)

Watching for their opportunity, the leaders sent spies pretending to be honest men. They tried to get Jesus to say something that could be reported to the Roman governor so he would arrest Jesus. "Teacher," they said, "we know that you speak and teach what is right and are not influenced by what others think. You teach the way of God truthfully. Now tell us is it right for us to pay taxes to Caesar or not?" He saw through their trickery and said, "Show me a Roman coin. Whose picture and title are stamped on it?" "Caesar's, "they replied. "Well then," he said, "give to Caesar what belongs to Caesar, and give to God what belongs to God." So they failed to trap him by what he said in front of the people. Instead, they were amazed by his answer, and they became silent. (Luke 20:20-26 NLT)

Therefore, thinking like Jesus and asking yourself: "What would Jesus do" will not result in the softest, cowardly response or action. It will, instead, result in the most amazing, unbelievable response or action as God intends every time. We ought to think like Christ always, in every situation of our lives.

Let this mind be in you, which was also in Christ Jesus. (Philippians 2:5 KJV)

You may be asking yourself what thinking like Christ means. What we need to know here is simply what was the mind of Christ Jesus? Sure, no one knew every thought of Jesus Christ –no one but God the Father. But what we do know are Christ's actions. As stated earlier our actions are the results of our thoughts. Therefore, based on Jesus' actions, we can conclude what He thought. With that being said, I think it's safe to say that the first and most important thing that was on the mind of Jesus Christ was always the will of God the Father.

For I have come down from heaven to do the will of God who sent me, not to do my own will. (John 6:38 NLT)

Jesus was selfless; His objective was not to do what pleased or benefited Him. He was all about His Father's business. Jesus' whole perspective was about glorifying God the Father and reconciling the relationship between God and humanity. Let's take a look at the crucifixion of Jesus Christ. Jesus, like many of us who live righteous lives, may have been thinking: "Here I am sinless, yet, dying on a cross for human beings who are full of sin. Not only am I dying for them, but these very people are killing Me, crucifying Me, spitting on Me, mocking, and laughing at Me. Why should I go through this for them? I'm too good; I don't deserve this. After all, they don't even appreciate what I'm doing for them. Let Me get off this cross and let them pay for their sins. After all, they committed the sins and deserve this, not Me." Instead, this is what happened:

> *Though he was God, he did not think of equality with God as something to cling to. Instead, he gave up his divine privileges; he took the humble position of a slave and was born as a human being. When he appeared in human form, he humbled himself in obedience to God and died a criminal's death on a cross.* (Philippians 2:6-8 NLT)

I don't care what life experiences you've suffered, no one has suffered like Jesus Christ. He didn't deserve any of His persecutions but He endured them all for us. Jesus' perspective was the total opposite of what some of ours would have been. He wasn't even a factor in the scheme of things. Rather, His mind was on humanity and God the Father redeeming our relationship by any means necessary, hence, His purpose. Yes, He asked that God the Father would take the pain away:

> *"Abba, Father,"* he cried out, *"everything is possible for you. Please take this cup of suffering away from me. Yet I want your will to be done, not mine."* (Mark 14:36 NLT)

But because His focus was on fulfilling the will of the Father, He said: "Nevertheless, not my will but thy will be done." Pleasing the Father was always on the mind of Christ. Jesus didn't spend time thinking of ways to be popular, famous or even liked. He didn't even spend time thinking about what He would eat, drink, wear or live. What I'm saying is Jesus' status was not the most significant part of His existence. He lived to do His Father's will and the Father always supplied His needs. What does that tell us? We need to stop thinking and worrying about our status and material things that cloud our minds. Our attention should be shifted to what's really important – doing the Father's will.

> *"So don't worry about these things, saying, "What will we eat? What will we drink? What will we wear? These things dominate the thoughts of unbelievers, but your heavenly Father already knows all your needs. Seek the Kingdom of God above all else, and live righteously, and he will give you everything you need.* (Matthew 6:31-33 NLT)

Think on and do the things that will please God our Father. What are the things that please God our Father?

> *Be careful to obey all my commands, so that all will go well with you and your children after you, because you will be doing what is good and pleasing to the Lord your God.* (Deuteronomy 12:28 NLT)

> *Thou shalt have no other gods before me. Thou shalt not make unto thee any graven image, or any likeness of anything that is in heaven above, or that is in the earth beneath, or that is in the water under the earth: Thou shalt not bow down thyself to them, nor serve them: for I the Lord thy God am a jealous God, visiting the iniquity of the fathers upon the children unto the third and fourth generation of them that hate me; and shewing mercy unto thousands of them that love me, and keep my commandments. Thou shalt not take the name of the Lord thy God in vain; for the Lord will not hold him guiltless that taketh his name in vain. Remember the Sabbath day, to keep it holy. Six days shalt thou labour, and do all thy work: but the seventh day is the Sabbath of the Lord thy God: in it thou shalt not do any work, thou, nor thy son, nor thy daughter, thy manservant, nor thy cattle, nor thy stranger that is within thy gates; For in six days the Lord made heaven and earth, the sea, and all that in them is, and rested the seventh day; wherefore the Lord blessed the Sabbath day, and hallowed it. Honor thy father and thy mother; that thy days may be long upon the land which the Lord thy God giveth thee. Thou shalt not kill. Thou shalt not commit*

adultery. Thou shalt not steal. Thou shalt not bear false witness against thy neighbor. Thou shalt not covet thy neighbor's house, thou shalt not covet thy neighbor's wife, nor his manservant, nor his maidservant, nor his ox, nor his ass, nor anything that is thy neighbor's. (Exodus 20:3-17 KJV)

I know you might be saying it's too hard to do all of that; no one in this world can obey all of God's commandments. I would say that you're right; we cannot obey all of God's commandments on our own. We can't even obey one of God's commandments on our own. We need the help of the Holy Spirit who is God living inside of us to accomplish this. Most importantly, it's the Holy Spirit who changes our hearts and gives us the desire to obey God's commandments even though we may mess up from time to time. God sees our hearts.

I can do all things through Christ which strengtheneth me.
(Philippians 4:13 KJV)

When we live our lives according to God's purpose, the things of this world can't hinder us. I believe one of the reasons Jesus' status didn't matter to Him was not because He was antisocial and didn't care about being liked. But because He knew this earth was not His home. Sometimes, I think we get caught up in the things of this world so much that we forget that it's not our home either. Sometimes, we live like it is. Why do I say that? Ever heard the saying "you only live once" or "I'ma ride this train til the wheels fall off"? These sayings lead us to believe that there is no life after this and that there's nothing beyond this earth so we had better make the most of it while we're here.

But we know that's false because the Word of God tells us in Colossians 3:2 NLT to, "Think about the things of heaven, not the things of earth."

But we are citizens of heaven where the Lord Jesus Christ lives. And we are eagerly waiting for him to return as our savior. (Philippians 3:20 NLT)

Our lives go beyond this earth. Jesus understood that. If we could also understand that truth and apply it to our lives, we would be much better off in every area of our lives.

Imagine not having to worry or stress about anything in life. Imagine simply leaning and depending on God who's in control and all powerful in every situation. You just live each day doing what God created you to do. This is the way we ought to live. However, the reality is we don't do this all of the time. Let's be honest: we don't even do this most of the time. It's not that we don't trust God, but we don't always use the Christ mindset. Scripture tells us:

> *For, who can know the Lord's thoughts? Who knows enough to teach him? But we understand these things, FOR WE HAVE THE MIND OF CHRIST.* (1 Corinthians 2:16 NLT emphasis added)

We have been given the ability to think like Christ but when we choose to, we don't use that ability. What happens when we don't use the mind of Christ? To answer that question, let's look first at what happens when we do use the mind of Christ. To put it simply, we get supernatural results. They may not happen overnight, but they are sure to happen when we think like Christ. The mind of Christ is the mind of the One who knows all. Therefore, His thoughts and His ways are already in accordance with what He knows will be the victorious end. Our minds are limited, and sometimes, we have no idea what's going to happen. So sometimes, we think in panic mode instigated by fear. This pretty much always leads to the wrong thoughts, which lead to the wrong actions, which lead to catastrophic results.

Therefore, when we don't use the mind of Christ, we get natural or sometimes catastrophic outcomes. In God's mind, He has a plan and a purpose for everyone and everything. His plan and purpose are driven by His love and care for us all. There is nothing on this earth that God does not care about. His actions prove His love.

> *And if God cares so wonderfully for wildflowers that are here today and thrown into the fire tomorrow, he will certainly care for you. Why do you have so little faith?* (Matthew 6:30 NLT)

Imagine if we too would look at everything and everyone with the same value and purpose God does. We would treat people and things a whole lot better. We wouldn't just love and care for those who reciprocate those feelings but we would love and care for all people and everything. If we use the mind of Christ, we wouldn't spend as much time on the plan of a thing as we would on the purpose of a thing. When we spend too much time on the plan, the carnal mind and its ideas kick in. But when we seek God on the purpose for the thing, He leads us to care for it with the love of Christ. I think this is a good time for me to share my story to better help you understand what I'm talking about. Though I'm sure most religious people would disagree with me for sharing this, I understand the power of our testimonies.

> *And they have defeated him by the blood of the Lamb and by their testimony. And they did not love their lives so much that they were afraid to die.* (Revelation 12:11 NLT)

I understand that God has forgiven me, and He is my vindicator. Therefore, if sharing my story causes persecution from religious folks, but it helps someone to begin or restore his or her relationship with God and keep them from doing something outside of the will of God, then so be it.

At age 19, I found myself at a place where I never thought I would be. I was in a long-term relationship. Look at this, 19 years old and in a long-term relationship (the only relationship I should have been in was with Jesus Christ). I'm not putting an age appropriate limit on a relationship or marriage here. What I'm simply saying is that the FIRST relationship anyone should have is with God. Once your relationship with God is in order and healthy, then you are ready to be in a relationship with another (courtship). The age for this varies from person to person. For me, at age 19, I needed to focus on my relationship with God; it was developing at that time. However, it wasn't solid enough for me to be in a relationship and live holy especially being in a relationship with the person I was with. It didn't help make my relationship with God any better.

At that time, I thought as long as I had Jesus too having a "boo" wouldn't harm me. Boy was I wrong. There I was at age 19, where I never thought I would be. I entered the relationship with every intention to live holy and keep God first in my life. At the beginning of our relationship, I told my boyfriend at the time that I loved the Lord and because of that, I wanted to do what He asks of me. That meant no sex before marriage. Of course, he was not happy with this arrangement, but he told me he wanted to be with me so, "Ok, I have to wait." And wait he did – but not until marriage. This, by the way, is in direct violation of the will of God; I'm just sharing my story.

To make a long story short, I was 19 and pregnant. All that went through my mind were the carnal things. "He isn't my husband; we can't take care of a child in any way – financially, emotionally or any "ly" for that matter." Every thought that could run through my mind to tell me why I couldn't have that baby did. Even down to my own childhood memories and what I wanted and couldn't have. Thoughts that the same thing would be true for my child consumed my mind. I thought about how I was going to raise this child. With my physical eyes, I couldn't see a plan. In my mind, it was impossible for me to birth that child and give him or her a better life than I had. Looking at the plan or the lack thereof, I couldn't go through with the pregnancy.

At 19 years old, I had an abortion. It was something I knew was wrong and never thought I would do. Having sex before marriage and certainly, having an abortion was wrong then, and will be wrong if you do them now; they will always be wrong in the sight of God. The saddest thing was, I knew my actions were wrong, and I still went through with them. Why? Not because I didn't love or trust God but because I wasn't thinking with the mind of Christ; I was thinking carnally. I had already messed up by having sex before marriage but that didn't mean that the baby I was carrying had no purpose. Had I thought with the mind of Christ, first of all, I wouldn't have been in a relationship at that time to make that mistake. But aside from that, once I had already messed up, I wouldn't have been so focused on the plan to take care of the child as if I was my own provider anyway – God is. Instead, I would have thought about the purpose God had for that child, and I would not have dared to interfere with it.

Chapter 3 • Guarding Your Mind

For to be carnally minded is death; but to be spiritually minded is life and peace. Because the carnal mind is enmity against God: for it is not subject to the law of God, neither indeed can be. (Romans 8:6-7 KJV)

You can't think spiritually once you've allowed the carnal to take over your mind. What do I mean by this? As I've stated, I didn't have the abortion because I didn't love or trust God (spiritual). I had it because I allowed my carnal mind to take over, bombarding me with every realistic, negative thought I could think of when I should have been using the mind of Christ in the situation.

For all have sinned, and come short of the glory of God. (Romans 3:23 KJV)

The point being made is that when we are thinking carnally, trusting God isn't even a factor. Thinking carnally makes things like trusting God, believing God, and having faith in God nonexistent or not even a thought or option. Therefore, because I was not using the mind of Christ those spiritual principles, values, and truths could not even get into my mind to come into play. This is why it's so important for us to use the mind of Christ and not our carnal minds based on our intellect. We know nothing but God knows everything.

If you are reading this book, and you're a Christian or just familiar with gospel music, I'm sure you have heard of gospel artist, Israel Houghton. If you have, you may have heard his story. His mother (a white woman) got pregnant with him at age 17 by his black father. During that time (1971), the society was segregated. Therefore, when his mother told her parents that she was pregnant by a black man, they suggested an abortion. Had she used her carnal mind because of the circumstances she was facing, what they said would have made a lot of sense. However, thank God, she didn't. If she had gone through with the abortion, the world would have missed the gifted songs God placed in Israel.

One of the things that made it most difficult for me to forgive myself and the question that played over and over in my mind was: "What gift to God's kingdom did I abort?" Had I just thought of the purpose for that child even in my sin, I would have kept him or her.

But I didn't think of this because I didn't use the mind of Christ; I thought carnally.

There maybe someone reading this right now who like me made the same mistake. You aborted a child, maybe even a ministry or something God desired to birth through you. You allowed it to die. Like me, you may have known it was wrong but you still went through with it because you had no clue what you were really doing. I want to speak to you right now. First of all, what you did wasn't a surprise to God (the one who knows all); it was a surprise to you. Much like me, I'm sure you never thought you would have done what you did. If you're anything like me, you even said you would never do such a thing before you did it. I want you to know we are not alone. Peter declared,

> *"Even if everyone else deserts you, I will never desert you." Jesus replied, "I tell you the truth, Peter this very night, before the rooster crows, you will deny three times that you even know me."* (Matthew 26:33-34 NLT)

"I will never deny you, Lord," Peter said. I'm sure at the time he said it, he really meant it from the bottom of his heart. However, the Lord already knew Peter would deny him before he declared he never would. So don't beat up yourself about the mistakes you've made or the sins you've committed. Repent, turn from that sin and the way you thought that caused you to do what you did. Remember, all have sinned and fallen short of the glory of God. But I know the Enemy is still tormenting you about your past so let's pray your way to freedom in Christ right now. Repeat this prayer:

> *Father God, in the name of Jesus, this sin I've committed (voice it) came as no surprise to You. But it shocked the life out of me. I am deeply sorry for committing this sin and because I know I shouldn't have done it but I did anyway, I didn't even feel worthy to come to You for forgiveness. I almost felt like I should pay for what I did because I knew it was wrong before I did it. But I thank You, Lord, that You already knew I would mess up before I did and You sent Your Son Jesus Christ to die for my sins over 2,000 years ago. I realize Father that Jesus' blood was enough; I don't have to pay for my sins because Jesus already did. I thank You, Lord, that*

You've been waiting for this moment, for this prayer for me to give this to You and move forward with my life. Lord, I ask for Your forgiveness, and I receive Your forgiveness. Help me to forgive myself and others for all of the sins we have committed especially those that we never thought we would. You so graciously wait for us to learn how to use the mind of Christ. In Jesus' name, I pray. Amen.

God is not waiting for you to sin and mess up so He can punish you and make you feel unworthy of His love. He loves you so much that He has already covered all of your sins past, present, and future under the blood of His Son Jesus.

For God presented Jesus as the sacrifice for sin. People are made right with God when they believe that Jesus sacrificed his life, shedding his blood. This sacrifice shows that God was being fair when he held back and did not punish those who sinned in times past. (Romans 3:25 NLT)

God is waiting for you to let this mind be in you, which was also in Christ Jesus (Philippians 2:5 KJV) so that He can use you to fulfill the purpose He created you for. Therefore, we live and learn; we use our life experiences to help us to think like Christ in every situation. So brethren, let's get our minds right. How? By doing what the Word of God tells us.

Finally, brethren, whatsoever things are true, whatsoever things are honest, whatsoever things are just, whatsoever things are pure, whatsoever things are lovely, whatsoever things are of good report; if there be any virtue, and if there be any praise, think on these things. (Philippians 4:8 KJV)

Let these things help us continue using the mind of Christ.

Chapter 4

GUARDING YOUR HEART

Guard your heart above all else, for it determines the course of your life. (Proverbs 4:23 NLT)

The above scripture clearly explains why the Enemy attacks your heart. For it says: "Your heart determines the course of your life. If you didn't know before reading this book, I think you know by now that the Enemy's course for your life is death and destruction with him. Therefore, his purpose for attacking your heart is to ultimately get you to harden your heart toward God, reject God and follow the Enemy to death. The Enemy's primary strategy is to keep your heart unclean so that you won't love the way that God wants you to. He neither wants you to display nor receive God's love. As a result, the revelation of the love of God throughout the world will be disrupted and it will keep people from drawing close to God.

Most important of all, continue to show deep love for each other, for love covers a multitude of sins. (1 Peter 4:8 NLT)

God is love; we can't be His children or say we even know Him if we don't love.

But anyone who does not love does not know God, for God is love. (1 John 4:8 NLT)

This is why the Enemy tricks people out of loving whether they know it or not. He uses situations in our lives to turn us from loving to hating. How so? As God tells us in His Word, we will have hard times in life.

> *I have told you all this so that you may have peace in me. Here on earth you will have many trials and sorrows. But take heart, because I have overcome the world.* (John 16:33 NLT)

Although God allows those hard times for one purpose, the Enemy tries to use them for the opposite. For instance, orphans who grew up with the pain of not knowing or having their birth parents in their lives. God desires that they use their experiences to better the lives of their children giving them the love and life they wanted but didn't have growing up.

On the other hand, the Enemy wants those orphans to be so angry because they didn't have the love of their birth parents that they take it out on their children by not showing them any love so they could feel their pain. The same goes for every other type of relationship. God wants us to learn and grow from our experiences but the Enemy wants us to focus on the negatives, become angry and make life difficult for those who are innocent of wrongdoing.

For most people, love is what comes to mind when they hear the word "heart." However, when I hear that word, I immediately think about life. It's the heart that possesses the life. When the heart of a person stops beating, life ends. The heart beat is the drive, the passion and what motivates and keeps life going. However, the interesting thing is that a person's heartbeat or passion can be either good or evil. The heart of a person determines which path of the life journey he or she will live out – good or evil. Ask yourself which path of life you will travel. Will it be the road of good or of evil?

Basically, what you are living for is what determines what you fill your heart with to keep it beating; for the purpose you intend to live to pursue good or evil. Because God loves us so much, He will show us our hearts and give us the chance to change what needs to be changed. When God shows you your heart, don't reject what He reveals. Or think that you can just ignore the things that you need to get rid of that He's showing you and just try not to fill your heart with it again. No, acknowledge what God is showing you in your heart (which stems from evil), don't ignore it, repent, and ask Him to deliver you from it and help you not to allow it into your heart again.

Why don't we acknowledge the wrongs in our hearts when God brings them to our attention? Be honest. There are several reasons why we don't, but I think the biggest and most dangerous one is PRIDE. When God shows us the wrong in our hearts all we tend to see is: WE ARE WRONG. For most of us, this is hard to accept, though we know we are human and we are liable to make mistakes; we just don't like to be wrong. Instead of admitting we're wrong at the time we're exposed, we think it's easier to let our pride rule and just ignore fixing our wrongdoings. We just make sure that we don't make that error again. But this way of living is not good according to the Word of God.

> *If another believer sins against you, go privately and point out the offense. If the other person listens and confesses it, you have won that person back. But if you are unsuccessful, take one or two others with you and go back again, so that everything you say may be confirmed by two or three witnesses. If the person still refuses to listen, take your case to the church. Then if he or she won't accept the church's decision, treat that person as a pagan or a corrupt tax collector.* (Matthew 18:15-17 NLT)

> *Dear brothers and sisters, if another believer is overcome by some sin, you who are godly should gently and humbly help that person back onto the right path. And be careful not to fall into the same temptation yourself.* (Galatians 6:1 NLT)

God wants us to address our sins, fix the issues at hand through Him and then move forward. This is how we grow and keep the Enemy under our feet. It also reminds us and the Enemy that we need God; we are nothing and can do nothing without Him. In our own strength, we will mess up. It's by the Spirit of God and God's grace that we are able to live pleasing and acceptable lives in the sight of God. We depend on and look to Him for everything including the building of our character. We are and can do nothing without God.

> *Yes, I am the vine; you are the branches. Those who remain in me, and I in them, will produce much fruit. For apart from me you can do nothing.* (John 15:5 NLT)

People's actions, their works, and the things they do are often reflections of what is in their hearts. But only God truly knows what's in a man's heart. God left us examples of other men and women of God so we can look at the condition of their hearts and what happened to them to help us on our Christian journeys. David, a man after God's heart is a prime example:

> *And when he had removed him, he raised up unto them David to be their king; to whom also he gave testimony, and said, I have found David the son of Jesse, a man after mine own heart, which shall fulfil all my will.* (Acts 13:22 KJV)

There are so many great things to be said about David, but there are also some things that he's remembered for that aren't so great. David committed a sin I'm sure he never thought he would have done. He slept with another man's wife and got her pregnant. Then he had her husband killed after she got pregnant. After committing these deeds, he married the woman to cover up his sin (read 2 Samuel Chapters 11 & 12 for the full story). Surely, his actions didn't come from a heart that was after God. There was nothing godly about his behavior; he knew she was married. Therefore, he should have left her alone, to begin with. But he didn't use the mind of Christ; he used his carnal mind and followed the lust of his flesh. It resulted in catastrophe with the murder of an innocent man.

It's evident that David never thought he would have committed such a sin. In 2 Samuel 12:1-5 when Nathan revealed David's sin in a parable, David didn't recognize his own sin. He was furious at the sinner in Nathan's story. He vowed: "Any man who would do such a thing deserves to die!" But what happened next was what God was waiting for to restore David. He expects the same from us when we mess up, to restore us. After David made this vow, Nathan rebuked David and told him that he was the man in the story; then David REPENTED of his sin. Nathan told him the Lord had forgiven him and he won't die for that sin. What an awesome God we serve!

What I find to be so amazing is not just God's forgiveness but what He said. I bet you probably missed it the first time just as I did. When David repented, Nathan said, "Yes, but the Lord has forgiven you, and you won't die for this sin." I want to really look at this last sentence, and I pray you really see the grace and mercy of our God in it. "And you won't die for this sin." Here is the eye opener: sin is designed to lead to death.

> *For the wages of sin is death, but the free gift of God is eternal life through Christ Jesus our Lord.* (Romans 6:23 NLT)

The definition of sin is – an immoral act considered to be a transgression against divine law. It's no secret that our sins keep us separated from God. "It's your sins that have cut you off from God. Because of your sins, He has turned away and will not listen anymore" (Isaiah 59:2 NLT). The bottom line is that the Enemy tries to keep us in sin, to keep us separated from God, to lead us to death – with him. Though God can't look upon our sins, when we repent, He forgives us and we're no longer separated from Him by that sin. Do you see why we must acknowledge our sins and repent and why we can't allow our pride to make us ignore sin? God doesn't reveal our sins to show us how unworthy we are to be in fellowship with Him. He exposes our sins so we will repent and be restored to fellowship with Him.

Most people who know to do right and that they should be living for the Lord, don't. Why? Because they misunderstand the meaning of the term; "our sins keep us separated from God." They have the mindset that it's too hard to live holy because everyone sins and once you sin, it's over. But that's a lie! God doesn't make it any easier for us to live holy and be in a relationship with Him. My brothers and sisters, the hardest thing to enable us to live holy and be in a relationship with God was already done on the cross. Jesus died to rekindle our relationship with God. God knows we will mess up; that's why He blessed us with His grace and mercy. When we repent, He forgives us, and because He knows our hearts, He even helps us by His spirit not to commit that sin again; it doesn't get any better than that folks. For those of you who have been misguided by the lie that because of your sins you can't come to God, let's pray right now against that deceptive spirit. But before we do that here's a scripture you should know:

For it is by grace you have been saved, through faith and this is not from yourselves, it is the gift of God not by works, so that no one can boast. (Ephesians 2:8-9 NIV)

Father God, in the name of Jesus, I recognize that all this time I've been tricked by the Enemy into believing that I couldn't have a relationship with You because I'm a sinner. But I thank You for the realization that all were born into sin but through Your Son Jesus, our sins are cleansed and we now have a right to a relationship with You. I now realize that it's this lie of perfection that I must be perfect to come to You that has kept me from coming near to You, the perfect and excellent God. I thank You that it's by Your grace that I'm saved. For You said in Your Word in Ephesians 2:8-9 NLT: "For it is by grace you have been saved, through faith-and this is not from yourselves, it is the gift of God not by works, so that no one can boast." By Your Holy Spirit, You will help me to conquer my sins. I place my sins at Your feet; forgive me, Father, and help me not to commit them again so I won't be separated from You. And if ever I am again, keep me from pride when You show me my sins so I will repent and be restored to a right standing and fellowship with You. In Jesus' name, I pray. Amen!

Some of us are tormenting ourselves over what we may think is one big sin we committed. In this one instance, David committed two horrible sins; first, he committed adultery, then he murdered the innocent man whose wife he stole. But the moment he repented, he was forgiven by God. Don't get me wrong. David didn't just utter the words, "I'm sorry Lord" or "I repent." He meant it from his heart; he had godly sorrow. Don't get it twisted folks; God knows your heart; therefore, He knows when you're sincerely repenting. God is neither mocked nor is He ignorant; there are consequences for our sins. Those consequences aren't to punish us but to teach and keep us from sinning. In this instance, the

Lord forgave David. However, one of the consequences of his sin was that the child he had with Bathsheba in an ungodly way died. But God our Father is good; He blessed David and Bathsheba with another son whom the Lord loved and even named after him (being loved by the Lord).

No one is perfect. Therefore, perfection isn't what makes a heart after God. If it did, we would probably think that we don't need God. We would rely on our own perfection, not God or anyone else for that matter. What makes a heart after God is a repentant heart. It's a heart that is in tune with the Holy Spirit and humble enough to repent when God exposes the ills within. He does this so that after repentance, God can clean and turn your heart around; He can use you for His purpose. That's the heart that David possessed.

God blesses those whose hearts are pure, for they will see God.
(Matthew 5:8 NLT)

David, like all of us, made mistakes – horrible mistakes. But when God exposed him, he didn't allow pride to get in the way and reject the correction sent to him. He realized in that moment that he had given into his carnal nature and he repented. God forgave him and continued to use him as if the sin he committed never occurred. David was a human being like us; He committed sin because his heart was fed with the wrong thing at the time. He was consumed by the lust of his flesh. Anytime your heart is filled with anything ungodly, it will lead to death.

A peaceful heart leads to a healthy body; jealousy is like cancer in the bones. (Proverbs 14:30 NLT)

When David saw Bathsheba, he was not where he was supposed to be. He had stayed behind in Jerusalem when he was supposed to be at war. It was at that time when he was on the roof, he noticed Bathsheba bathing and he lusted after her.

To guard your heart, you need to be where God wants you to be, doing what He ordains. Don't be idle; it gives much room for the Enemy to play with your mind, get to your heart, lead you to do the wrong things and then destroy you. Many believe that because America is a free country, those of us who live here can be wherever we want to be. In a way that's true; however, when you belong to God there are strings attached. As children of God (the lights of the world), we are called to specific people, places, and things. In Christianity, we call this being on assignment for the Lord.

At these assignments, we are to reach those God has called us to, do what He has called us to do there, and keep moving forward as He leads. We must also continue to grow in Him and help others to do the same – expanding God's kingdom. When we are not in or at our assignments, we are off track and outside of God's will. Therefore, we are unable to get all that we need to grow in Him. As a result, we become prey to the Enemy's tricks and tactics and fall into sin. For example, the Bible clearly tells us to assemble ourselves together:

> *And let us consider and give attentive, continuous care to watching over one another, studying how we may stir up (stimulate and incite) to love and helpful deeds and noble activities, not forsaking or neglecting to assemble together [as believers], as is the habit of some people, but admonishing (warning, urging, and encouraging) one another, and all the more faithfully as you see the day approaching.* (Hebrews 10:24-25 AMPC)

I've heard of many who proclaim to be Christians who state they don't nor do they need to fellowship with other Christians; specifically in church fellowships. They state they pray and read their Bibles at home. This is good that they do this however, let me state that I don't believe this instruction to "not forsake or neglect to assemble together [as believers]" was limited to church fellowships. These meetings can take place anywhere with any group of believers of Christ. The purpose of our meeting together is certainly to praise and worship God. But it's also to encourage one another and watch over each other. Therefore, of course we are all held accountable to God but God also holds us accountable to one another. If not this Scripture would not tell us to watch over one another.

Yes David was King and he should have been held as accountable to his people; as I'm sure they were held accountable to him. If David was where he was supposed to be – at war fighting with his people – he would never have seen Bathsheba bathing to lust after her. He would not have been tempted to commit adultery. I'm not saying that going or not going to a Christian fellowship saves you or that not being a part of a Christian fellowship makes you unsaved. I am well aware that there are seasons in our lives where God may actually remove us from the physical church building/fellowship and set us apart for consecration to him for a while. If and when this season comes in one's life it is to draw the individual closer to God not away from him. What I'm talking about are those Christians who feel they NEVER need to be a part of a Christian fellowship of some sort throughout their entire Christian journey.

I have a question for those who feel like they don't need to fellowship with other believers of Christ to be successful or fulfill their Christian duties to the fullest; throughout their Christian journey. When you're not fellowshipping with other believers, where are you? Are you somewhere feeding your flesh or your spirit? Remember, I stated earlier, what you're living for determines what you fuel or feed your heart (yourself) with. This leads to my second point on guarding your heart. To guard your heart you must protect your eyes and ears; what you allow yourself to see and hear will feed you. Ever notice how you feel after you've watched a particular film or listened to certain music? I've noticed when I listened to violent music or even watched films with violence in them that all of a sudden, I wanted to fight. After the film, I found myself all riled up, and if you said the wrong thing to me at that time you were liable to get it (lol)! But seriously, if you're feeding your eyes with the lust of your flesh then that's what will fill your heart. If you don't want to fill your heart with violence then don't watch violence. If you don't want to fill your heart with lust, don't watch sexually explicit shows and so forth.

I want to better help you understand the importance of a healthy heart – a heart after God, on your Christian journey. To do so, let's dissect the natural heart and its functions in the human body. I want to talk about an unhealthy heart in the natural, what causes it, and where those unhealthy things lead the heart to. Let's look at atherosclerosis for example:

> *Heart disease includes numerous problems, many of which are related to a process called Atherosclerosis. Atherosclerosis is a condition that develops when a substance called plaque builds up in the walls of the arteries. This buildup narrows the arteries, making it harder for blood to flow through. If a blood clot forms, it can stop the blood flow. This can cause a heart attack or stroke. A heart attack occurs when the blood flow to a part of the heart is blocked by a blood clot.* (Cardiovascular disease/American Heart Association)

In the spiritual realm, I can imagine the hardened heart as atherosclerosis and our sins as the plaque buildup. As we learned from David's situation, God our Father is so loving and kind that He will show us our hearts and the sins we are committing so we can repent and turn our hearts back to Him. However, if unlike David, we are not sorry for our sins when God shows them to us, our hearts will not be pure and clean. All of the buildup of our sins will turn into spiritual plaque that will narrow the arteries making it harder for the Spirit of God's living water to flow through us. If the Spirit of God cannot flow freely through us, the buildup of our sins will block the blood from flowing to our hearts. The refusal to repent of our sins will harden our hearts and lead to a spiritual heart attack.

A heart attack is any sudden instance of heart failure (*Webster's New World Dictionary*). Let's look at what the dictionary says the heart itself is. It says: "The heart is the hollow, muscular organ that circulates the blood by alternate dilation and contraction, the central, vital, or main part; core, the human heart considered as the center of emotions, personality attributes, etc. in most thought and feeling love, sympathy, etc. spirit or courage, a conventionalized design of a heart." (*Webster's New World Dictionary*).

When you have a spiritual heart attack, you are spiritually dead. This simply means that you are dead to the things of the spirit and totally alive and available to the things of the flesh (darkness).

> *Be careful then, dear brothers and sisters. Make sure that your own hearts are not evil and unbelieving, turning you away from the living God.* (Hebrews 3:12 NLT)

Remember, I said earlier that our heart beat is our passion or drive. If our heart is filled with evil, we will commit evil. We know that God is nowhere in evil. However, if our hearts are filled with good and the principles of God, we'll see to it that we carry out His will and His ways. When our hearts are filled with evil, it turns us away from God. "The human heart is the most deceitful of all things, and desperately wicked. Who really knows how bad it is?" (Jeremiah 17:9 NLT). There are people who are doing good works and it looks like their hearts are full of good. They help people, are there for people and even pray for people. But it's so important for us to be in tune with God because we don't know their hearts, only God does.

Sometimes, people do good works for the wrong reasons. They want recognition or something in return. Their benevolence is not from their hearts or for godly reasons. Even evil hearts can do good deeds, but with the wrong motives. Your motives determine what your heart is filled with. So in this sinful world, how do we truly guard our hearts? We are human beings with thoughts, feelings, and experiences that affect our hearts. "How do we control the results of what will truly be the condition of our hearts? It's much simpler than you probably think. Of course, as I've stated, you have to guard your eyes and ears. Also, much like protecting our minds, we are going to see, hear, feel, and experience some things that if we had a choice we wouldn't because of the world we live in. Again, we don't have control over that, but we do have control over what we do with it.

Therefore, we can guard our hearts by checking in daily with the one who knows best – God the Father. Because of God's love when we mess up, He will show us our hearts but we should not wait until we mess up for God to reveal our true state. If we want to shield our hearts, we will check in with God daily as we pray for God to cleanse us. Another good way to do this is to pray this scripture daily:

Search me, O God, and know my heart; try me, and know my thoughts. Point out anything in me that offends you, and lead me along the path of everlasting life. (Psalms 139: 23-24 NLT)

In doing this, you are acknowledging your need for God. You are also opening up the communication for God to show you your heart so that you can repent where necessary and let your relationship with God be pure and genuine. This enables Him to fill your heart with the desire for good so He can freely use you for His service.

> *For God is working in you, giving you the desire and the power to do what please him.* (Philippians 2:13 NLT)

Another big thing that affects our hearts in a negative way is unforgiveness. The trickiest thing about unforgiveness is that most times, we don't even realize how much unforgiveness is in our hearts until it's rooted and grounded. It makes it much more difficult to get out. Do you realize that when you don't forgive, God can't forgive you?

> *If you forgive those who sin against you, your heavenly Father will forgive you. But if you refuse to forgive others, your Father will not forgive your sins.* (Matthew 6:14-15 NLT)

Forgiveness is crucial to living holy for other reasons as well. Jesus is the prime example of how forgiveness works. While He was being crucified, He asked God to forgive all of us for our sins (the past, present, and future) including the ones who were crucifying Him.

> *Jesus said, "Father, forgive them, for they don't know what they are doing."* (Luke 23:34 NLT)

If Jesus could forgive all of us including His enemies, certainly, we can forgive others for everything else. Just think about what you're doing when you don't forgive. You're basically judging the person and finding them not worthy of your forgiveness. But the last time I checked, the blood of Jesus qualified all of us for forgiveness. Additionally, unforgiveness causes you not to love the person or persons you choose not to forgive. What do you think your heart will be filled with if there is no love? Inevitably, it will be filled with hate. Therefore, to love as we ought to, we have to forgive.

I understand that forgiveness is not an easy thing to do. But the truth is God never said it would be easy; He said we have to do it. Remember, if we don't forgive each other then God can't forgive us. Because forgiveness is so crucial but for most so difficult, I think this is a good place to pray for strength in this area:

Father God, in the name of Jesus, I realize that if I don't forgive others for the wrongs they have and will do to me then You can't forgive me for the wrongs I've done. Lord, I need Your forgiveness, and I want to forgive those who have wronged me but I need Your help to do so. Lord, please empty me of all pride and fear of being hurt by those who've hurt me again and fill me with Your heart of forgiveness and compassion for them. Lift this heavy burden of unforgiveness and help me to freely forgive as You help my brothers and sisters do the same for me and all who have done them wrong. In Jesus' name, I pray Amen!

God always shows you what's in your heart that shouldn't be there. Nothing will build up inside of your heart to cause a spiritual heart attack if you take the proper precautions when God shows you your sins. Everything we do both good and evil comes from our hearts; that's why it is essential to guard our hearts on our Christian journey.

For from within, out of a person's heart, come evil thoughts, sexual immorality, theft, murder, adultery, greed, wickedness, deceit, lustful desires, envy, slander, pride, and foolishness. All these vile things come from within; they are what defile you." (Mark 7:21-23 NLT)

If we want to do good and not evil our hearts must be in the right place. There's no better way to examine our hearts than to check in with the examiner of all examiners, God the Father. He will reveal the problem and give you the grace to repent, fix, and guard your heart so you can truly live holy and be used by Him.

I tell you the truth, anyone who believes in me will do the same works I have done, and even greater works, because I am going to be with the Father. (John 14:12 NLT)

God the Father spoke the world into existence. However, He sent His Son Jesus into the earth (in the form of a human) for a reason. He needed a physical body, a vessel to dwell in and perform miracles to physically show us what we are to be and do here on the earth. God needs your heart to be clean so He can use you throughout the earth to do greater works than Jesus did. It's clear that He also needs your physical body to do this.

Chapter 5

GUARDING YOUR BODY

Don't you realize that your body is the temple of the Holy Spirit, who lives in you and was given to you by God? You do not belong to yourself, for God bought you with a high price. So you must honor God with your body. (1 Corinthians 6:19-20 NLT)

It's so important to the Enemy to attack your body, because you HONOR God with your body. The Enemy, of course, doesn't want you to honor God; he wants you to honor him by destroying your body because he wants to be your god. Therefore, he attacks your body to keep you from honoring God and from taking proper care of your body so that God can't use you for His dwelling, service, and glory; as he desires.

Your body is the temple of the Holy Spirit. To better understand this, think about the physical temples/churches of God we see, enter, and pass by every day. Whether you are spiritual, religious or not I think we share a similar definition or description of a temple/church of God. You would agree that back in the day, there was a certain respect and reverence for the temple/church of God that isn't as present today. People honored the temple of God from the outside in. If they walked past a church they would take inventory of their behavior and adjust it accordingly out of respect for the temple/church of God.

For instance, you wouldn't curse while passing a church building. You would put out your cigar before you got near and you wouldn't dare litter in the church or even around it. Certainly, people had the utmost respect and honor for the house of God. Men took off their hats or head coverings before entering. Children weren't allowed to play with or even touch the Bibles and hymn books; everything inside of the church was treated as sacred. I love how even today, those in the Catholic Church bow when entering the sanctuary before taking their seats, showing respect and honor to God.

I believe people treated the house of God this way because they viewed it as such, the house of God; the place where God dwelled and lived. Our bodies are the temples (houses) of God; therefore God lives in us. Scripture says because of this we must honor God with our bodies. The interesting thing about back in the day that differs from today is that people understood and respected this honor for the house of God, which we don't have today. Honor and reverence were seen as mandatory, not optional.

Although they may not have honored their physical bodies as the temples of God (just as we certainly don't today), they still honored and respected both the church building and the physical body more than most people do today.

They struggled with the same temptations and desires as we do but they weren't proud about their struggles. Actually, no one even knew of their struggles; they kept them hidden because of their respect for God's temple (their bodies). What am I saying? You didn't know a single woman from the church was sexually active until she got pregnant. Even then, out of respect for God's temple, in many cases, she got married before others knew she was pregnant.

Am I saying that their way of handling sex before marriage was right? No! I'm saying that with the same struggles and temptations we face today, they had more respect and honor for God's temple. They felt more convicted when they dishonored it than most people do today. These days, it appears to be the norm for singles to come to church proudly pregnant with no intention of getting married. It is also an advertisement of the person's sexual status, which they seem to enjoy; there is no shame, no respect or honor for the body as the temple of God. How do we do this? By advertising how many partners we had, how good they were, how good we are, and the entire layout of the experience.

Our bodies are temples of God. What does that mean to you? For those back in the day that meant a lot and as I said though they struggled with the same temptations and desires as we do today they handled those struggles with more respect and honor than we do today.

No matter what's our nationality, culture or family background most of us tidy our homes when we are expecting company. We clean up, prepare the entertainment, meals, and refreshments. Why do we do this? Because our homes are reflections of us. What people see when they visit, is usually a representation of who you are. They form opinions about what they see. If we keep our homes filthy they will view us as filthy. If we keep an unorganized home they will view us as unorganized. If our homes smell, they will be uncomfortable and most likely won't come back.

This is true in the natural, and it is also true in the spiritual. As children of God, we ought to look like and carry ourselves (our bodies) like the God we serve cares for and provides for us. Our bodies (God's temple) are reflections of our God. If we do not take care of our bodies; if we look a hot mess, unkempt, unwashed, and unhealthy, we are poor representations of the God we serve.

Have you ever been in a situation where a man or woman of God came to speak a word to you and you couldn't hear, far less receive it because of bad breath? Has someone ever tried to witness to you but their breath was so bad that you couldn't hear them? All you could hear were the voices in your head saying, "Jesus, heal him or her from that bad breath." If so, you would agree with me that taking care of your physical hygiene is important to witness and represent God effectively. If the believer who is witnessing is unkempt and has poor hygiene, the unbeliever won't want to be around that person or hear a word he or she has to say. I'm not saying you have to dress in the finest clothing or spend tons of money on the latest hairstyles, nails, accessories, etc. What I'm saying is don't walk around looking and smelling like you just rolled out of bed or the dumpster trying to witness. How will the unbelievers be persuaded that God provides when you look like you are homeless.

God is good; He provides for and takes good care of us. Therefore, how we look should be reflections of that. We ought to represent God well and guard our outer bodies by taking care of them. But what's most important is how we guard our inner bodies.

Our outer bodies are actually reflections of our inner bodies. Obesity, for instance, is an outright result and display of what we put into our bodies as well as how we treat our bodies (exercise, rest, etc.). Many of us abuse our temples, and we don't even know it. As Christians, we sometimes operate on auto-pilot doing any and everything for everyone else. We don't get enough rest or take care of ourselves, and we think we are doing the will of God. I always ask: "If God the Father took one day to rest, who do we think we are that we don't need to?" When we get too busy with life and don't allow our physical bodies to be cared for, we fall prey to the traps and snares of the Enemy. How so? We are not alert and on target.

> *So be on your guard, not asleep like the others. Stay alert and be clear-headed.* (1 Thessalonians 5:6 NLT)

Am I saying God will allow the Enemy to attack you even if your tiredness comes from doing the work of the Lord? Will God allow that to happen even though you believe He will give you the strength to do His work? Well, what I'm saying is obedience is better than sacrifice. God said to remember the Sabbath day and keep it holy.

> *You have six days each week for your ordinary work, but the seventh day is a Sabbath day of rest dedicated to the Lord your God. On that day no one in your household may do any work. This includes you, your sons and daughters, your male and female servants, your livestock, and any foreigners living among you.* (Exodus 20:9-10 NLT)

Why does God tell us to rest? In the natural, if you spent all day working to the point of exhaustion mentally and physically, and you were suddenly asked to take a general test on something you were taught, how do you think you would do? Do you think your mind would be alert? Would you be ready and fit to take the test? Would you be able to answer the question better if you were rested and refreshed? If a soldier fought day in and day out never taking a day to rest, how effective would he or she be during a war? The Enemy is out to tempt and trip us up all day, every day; all he needs is to catch us unalert and exhausted. We are sure to fail and cave into his tricks, traps, tactics, and temptations, which we probably would not have had we been more alert.

Without sufficient rest, you are not provided enough energy and fuel to accomplish the task set before you. It's almost like you are sleep walking, sleep talking, sleep working or sleep whatever activity you are doing. When you are sleep walking, you don't know what you're doing; your body is just moving without direction or understanding from your brain. Your body is functioning on auto-pilot with no thoughts or emotions behind it.

However, if we get the physical rest we need and if we are eating right, exercising and taking care of our bodies, we will make ourselves more available to God and others. We will be more alert and on guard in the natural and in the spiritual.

> *I discipline my body like an athlete, training it to do what it should. Otherwise, I fear that after preaching to others I myself might be disqualified.* (1 Corinthians 9: 27 NLT)

Don't misunderstand me; there is a difference between getting rest and just being lazy. I'm not talking about being lazy and just not doing the work of Christ while using rest as an excuse. I'm talking about resting where you allow your body to refuel so you can continue to do the work God has called you to do. No one can deny that after eating right, exercising, and getting the proper rest you feel better, more energized, stronger and you are more physically, mentally, and spiritually alert; you accomplish more. Have you ever tried to pray when you were exhausted or after you ate a big meal? How did that work out for you? Lol! Exactly! When we don't take care of our physical bodies, it affects us spiritually. We don't have the energy and fuel for our physical bodies to produce the things of the spirit in the natural such as prayer, studying the Word of God, and of course, our physical service to God and others.

I think it's safe to say that if we rest and take care of our bodies we are better off and of better use to ourselves and others.

> *It is useless for you to work so hard from early morning until late at night, anxiously working for food to eat; for God gives rest to his loved ones.* (Psalms 127:2 NLT)

It's not good to work yourself to exhaustion for the needs of others, and it's even worse to work yourself into exhaustion for yourself. Yes, we have to work hard to accomplish certain goals in life. For instance, if you're working toward a degree, weight loss or any tangible goal, it will require hard work. But what I'm saying is we need to be careful not to become obsessed with work trying to produce outcomes that we have no control over. God is in control; you do your part to reach your goal and let God do the rest. Don't work so hard trying to control matters that only God can. Basically, don't allow yourself to be so overcome by working for something or someone (physical labor), that you lose touch with what is most important – your time with God. Remember Mary and Martha!

> *As Jesus and the disciples continued on their way to Jerusalem, they came to a certain village where a woman named Martha welcomed him into her home. Her sister, Mary, sat at the Lord's feet, listening to what he taught. But Martha was DISTRACTED by the big dinner she was preparing. She came to Jesus and said, "Lord, doesn't it seem unfair to you that my sister just sits here while I do all the work? Tell her to come and help me." But the Lord said to her, "My dear Martha, you are worried and upset over all these details! There is only one thing worth being concerned about. Mary has discovered it, and it will not be taken away from her."* (Luke 10:38-42 NLT)

We are in spiritual warfare, but our physical bodies are the vessels and vehicles of God to be used by God. How can they be used if they are beaten down and burnt out? So we must take care of our physical bodies; by eating right, getting rest, exercising, and presenting them well put together before people. The Holy Spirit lives in you; He is a precious gift given to you by God to be cherished. Don't you want Him to feel comfortable inside of you?

People don't want others to get too comfortable in their homes when they are there at the wrong time or they don't want them to stay for a long period. Ya'll know that friend or family member you never invited over, to begin with who when they pop up, you can't wait for them to go home. In those cases, we purposely try to make them feel uncomfortable by hinting we're so tired or we have so much work to do that we start doing it while they're there (lol)! Forgive us, Lord.

But this shouldn't be the case with the Holy Spirit. Don't you want to make your body a place where the Holy Spirit can be comfortable to live, breathe, move, dwell and freely operate? Make your body a comfortable house for the Holy Spirit by monitoring what you allow to enter your temple, what you allow around your temple and where you take your temple. As I mentioned earlier, part of guarding your body is being selective about the foods you eat along with everything else that you put into your body. This includes cigarettes, drugs, weed, and alcohol. Many Christians have different views on these things. Some say Jesus turned water into wine so there's nothing wrong with drinking alcohol. Others say, weed is not a drug and God said every herb is good. I don't disagree with either of those things. Here's my theory:

Your body should not be controlled by any of these things. Neither should any of these things be used as your source of peace or joy. You ought to be controlled by the Holy Spirit and look to God for your peace, joy, and everything else you need.

> *Don't be drunk with wine, because that will ruin your life. Instead, be filled with the Holy Spirit.* (Ephesians 5:18 NLT)

> *Then each of you will control his own body and live in holiness and honor not in lustful passion like the pagans who do not know God and his ways.* (1 Thessalonians 4:4-5 NLT)

> *A person without self-control is like a city with broken down walls.* (Proverbs 25:28 NLT)

> *You will keep in perfect peace all who trust in you, all whose thoughts are fixed on you!* (Isaiah 26:3 NLT)

Do you find yourself in NEED of alcohol, cigarettes, weed, prescription and non-prescription drugs and other substances? Are you addicted and can't live without them? Do you use them hoping to get peace of mind? Or do they control you? If you find yourself being controlled by any of these things or anything other than the Holy Spirit for that matter, you have a problem.

Sometimes, guarding what's around your temple can be difficult. In many instances, we don't have control over the people and things surrounding us. We have to go about our day to day activities, which include working or going to school with people who don't carry themselves in the godliest ways. They may curse uncontrollably, play loud music you don't necessarily care to feed your spirit with and even wear clothing with statements and visuals you don't live by or want to see; sometimes, this is unavoidable. Remember, we live in this world but we are not of it; therefore, we can't expect unbelievers to live by our morals and standards; they are free to live according to their own. That's why we must cover ourselves daily in prayer under the blood of Jesus.

However, we do have control over where we take our temples in our free time. As I stated earlier, you are or you become what you feed yourself. Therefore, we should be careful to guard our bodies by refusing to take them to places where they are fed corruption. For example, if we take our bodies to the club where it's surrounded by sexually explicit music, sexual dancing, drugs, and alcohol, our flesh will crave those things. Clearly, those aren't the things God desires for us, and we make the Holy Spirit who dwells in us uncomfortable if we take him there.

For example, we wouldn't invite our street friends who smoke, drink alcohol, and take drugs into our homes to partake in such activities if our saved, sanctified, Holy Ghost filled, fire baptized grandmother was there, would we? No! It would not only make Grandma uncomfortable, but it would also be disrespectful to her. We should treat God our Father with even more respect than Grandma, and not allow ourselves to place the Holy Spirit in any uncomfortable position. I can hear somebody saying that Jesus went out into the highways and byways to save the lost; He didn't confine Himself to holy places. You are absolutely correct. However, are you going to the club, bar, or "highways and byways" to witness and save the lost as Jesus did? If not, then why exactly are you going there? And please, don't tell me to have a good time because I doubt very much that the Holy Spirit is enjoying Himself there.

It is not my intention to sound religious or unrealistic with a list of do's and don'ts, so let me try to better explain myself. I no longer go to clubs on weekends or just to have a good time as I did before I got serious about my walk with the Lord. Going to the club for the purpose I used to is no longer fun for me. I don't look to the club scene for a good time. However, I don't view the club as a "DO NOT ENTER ZONE" like if I go there I will burn in hell. If I have a family member or close friend who is hosting an event of importance at a club, I won't say I can't go because it's being held inside a club; that's religious thinking. Going inside a club doesn't make me any less of a Christian than if I don't go inside. However, if the Holy Spirit specifically tells me that I'm not to go there, no matter who is hosting the event, I won't go, no questions asked. The point I'm making is that the purpose for taking the Holy Spirit where we take Him is what's important. It should help with your decision to go or not to go.

> *Do not let any part of your body become an instrument of evil to serve sin. Instead, give yourselves completely to God, for you were dead but now you have new life. So use your whole body as an instrument to do what is right for the glory of God.* (Romans 6:13 NLT)
>
> *The path of the virtuous leads away from evil; whoever follows that path is safe.* (Proverbs 16:17 NLT)

Now, let's get to the good stuff; let's talk about sex. I'm sure when you looked at the title of this book, one of the first things you thought was: "I'm not reading that book because I'm not married. I love sex, and I don't want to be reminded that I'm really not supposed to be having it right now because I'm not married. I really have no desire to stop, and

I don't want to read anything to hinder my pleasure during intercourse." I'm such a good mind reader. Aren't I?

I prophesy to you right now in the name of Jesus that after reading this particular section you will have the understanding of God's view, intent, purpose, and stance on sex. You will desire to find and marry the person God has for you. You will stop having sex with that person you've been fornicating with in ignorance or just out of fear of commitment. Or you will go ahead and marry that person if he or she is the one God has for you; do it God's way. God created sex with the intention that it would be a special gift shared between a husband and a wife and for the purpose of populating the earth.

> *So God created human beings in his own image. In the image of God he created them; male and female he created them. Then God blessed them and said, "Be fruitful and multiply. Fill the earth and govern it. Reign over the fish in the sea, the birds in the sky, and all the animals that scurry along the ground."* (Genesis 1:27-28 NLT)

> *The husband should fulfill his wife's sexual needs, and the wife should fulfill her husband's needs.* (1 Corinthians 7:3 NLT)

He made it for our pleasure and enjoyment. If God didn't make sex feel good, we wouldn't do it and if we do not have sex, we can't populate the earth. Imagine if sex felt like exercise; there would probably only be five faithful people walking around on earth. I think you get my point. What's wrong with having sex before marriage if God put the sexual desire in us? Why would He want to torture us? How can He expect us to control our passions until marriage? Simply put, it's just not God's intention for you to experience sex before marriage. Sex is powerful and God made it to be a gift for marriage. Like any other power, if sex is used in the wrong way or for the wrong reason it can be dangerous. I've just stated some reasons why and how God created sex to be performed. If you're reading this book, and you're a non-believer or a new believer, you may not know this but let me inform you: The Enemy (Satan) was once in heaven. At that time, he was called Lucifer. He became proud and wanted to be worshiped

Chapter 5 • Guarding Your Body

and praised like God; he was kicked out of heaven by God because of his rebellion.

> *How art thou fallen from heaven, O Lucifer, son of the morning! How art thou cut down to the ground, which didst weaken the nations! For thou hast said in thine heart, I will ascend into heaven, I will exalt my throne above the stars of God: I will sit also upon the mount of the congregation, in the sides of the north: I will ascend above the heights of the clouds; I will be like the most High. Yet thou shalt be brought down to hell, to the sides of the pit.* (Isaiah 14:12-15 KJV)

Satan (Lucifer at the time) wanted and still wants to be God so he tries to imitate God, to get people to worship and serve him as God is worshiped and served. He even tried to get Jesus to bow down in worship to him. But Jesus said:

> *Again it is written, "You shall not put the Lord your God to the test. Again, the devil took him to a very high mountain and showed him all the kingdoms of the world and their glory. And he said to him, "All these I will give you, if you will fall down and worship me. Then Jesus said to him, "Be gone, Satan! For it is written, "You shall worship the Lord your God and him only shall you serve."* (Matthew 4:7-10 ESV)

If Satan tried Jesus, certainly, he will try you and me. Needless to say, Satan does this with sex as well. God has every good intention and purpose for sex between two married people, which is to bring them together to enjoy each other and multiply. But Satan uses God's good thing, to destroy, separate, and tear marriages apart, and to prevent marriage from even occurring. Certainly, as in my case, to stop the multiplication of humanity.

Satan activates the lustful spirits within us to look outside of our marriages to get what we are supposed to be getting in our marriages. I'm talking about cheating folks, which is one way most marriages are destroyed. God intended sex to be sacred, something shared between a husband and wife. When done God's way, there is no guilt or shame in having sex. You don't need to sneak around or look behind your shoulder to have sex with your husband or wife. You don't have to fear who's going to see you at the hotel with this or that person or if your secret will get out. When God blesses a husband and wife with conception there's joy in the family. Except in some cases where the couple has already been blessed with several children and are worried about their ability to support another child financially. But even then, abortion is normally not an option because the child is viewed as a blessing. They are not embarrassed because the child was conceived according to God's design. In these instances, pregnancy is still viewed as a blessing and other options like giving the child up for adoption to bless someone else may be considered.

On the other hand, in his attempt to be God, Satan takes sex, God's good thing, and makes it bad. For example, two unmarried people whether both are single or one married and one single. If you're a Christian and have any bit of the Holy Spirit within you, and you are having sex with someone other than your husband or wife you feel convicted. Sometimes, you are so guilt-stricken you can't even enjoy it. You sneak around to do it. Why? Because you know you're not supposed to be having sex with that person. And God forbid you end up pregnant or get someone pregnant; there's no joy. All you feel is embarrassment and shame, especially if the person you have conceived with is married to someone else. In this case, most times, abortion is the first and only option you have. Why? You were participating in sex, a godly act (for married people). But you did it out of God's context, against God's design. You indulged in fornication or committed adultery; by the way, Satan tricked you into it.

Say what you want to say. I've seen it time and time again where children (gifts from God) who were conceived outside of marriage don't receive the proper love or affection from their parents. These precious gifts are neglected because they were not conceived out of love but out of lust. Once the child's parent or parents find true love elsewhere, they get married and have more children in a loving relationship. The child see's the difference in the treatment and love that their parent or parents have for his or her siblings. Parents don't always do this on purpose. Actually, they may not even realize what's happening but the children notice and it affects them more than you know.

This is nothing new. We see a prime example of favoritism by a parent to a particular child in the case of Joseph and his brothers. The Bible says Jacob loved Joseph the most because he was born to him at his old age but I'm sure the fact that he was born through the woman he loved Rachel had something to do with it as well!

Since Jacob was in love with Rachel, he told her father, "I'll work for you for seven years if you'll give me Rachel, your younger daughter, as my wife". "Agreed!" Laban replied. "I'd rather give her to you than to anyone else. Stay and work with me." So Jacob worked seven years to pay for Rachel. But his love for her was so strong that it seemed to him but a few days. (Genesis 29:18-20 NLT)

So Jacob slept with Rachel, too, and he loved her much more than Leah. He then stayed and worked for Laban the additional seven years. (Genesis 29:30 NLT)

Jacob loved Joseph more than any of his other children because Joseph had been born to him in his old age. So one day Jacob had a special gift made for Joseph a beautiful robe. (Genesis 37:3 NLT)

But his brothers hated Joseph because their father loved him more than the rest of them. They couldn't say a kind word to him. (Genesis 37:4 NLT)

Can you imagine what life would be like if we experienced sex God's way? What would it be like if we were only allowed to have sex with our husbands or wives as God ordained? I don't believe there would be any cheating going on in the world. If we only had the option to have sex with our husbands or wives (God's way), there would be no reason to even entertain anyone else from the opposite sex. Whatever he or she has to offer would be nothing in comparison to what we get from our husbands or wives – the powerful gift of sex. You may say that's not necessarily true because emotional cheating is worse than the actual, physical act of cheating. Show me an affair that ended at the emotional cheating stage, and I'll agree with you. Exactly!!! The emotional cheating leads to the physical cheating – sex. Therefore, as I said, if sex with your husband or wife was the only option, there would be no need to entertain anyone else. Husbands and wives would love and appreciate each other and their marriages the way God intended them to.

One of the problems with sex before marriage is that the Enemy gives us variety on top of variety and confusion on top of confusion. For example, if an individual who has several sexual partners then decides that he or she is ready for marriage. The process of looking for a husband or wife begins. During this search, the individual may say: "This one makes me feel good but sex is better with that one. This one understands and supports me but with that one, sex is better." I can almost guarantee if sex is off the table before marriage the individual will more likely choose the better suited husband or wife. First of all, he or she will be handling the relationship God's way, which will help bring clarity and the ability to see the person for who they really are instead of what they can do in the bedroom. Love is not blind, great sex is! If you are having sex with someone who is not your husband or wife and the sex is great, that great sex will be all you see in him or her.

He or she could be going upside your head, stealing from you, using and abusing you and others

can see the person is no good for you but you won't see a thing wrong with them. Everything that is clear to those on the outside looking in, you will be blinded to by the great sex. And even if you do see the person is no good for you; you will find a way to justify their actions so you can continue to receive that great sex. However, there will come a time when you will see what everyone else on the outside saw the entire time but it may be much too late. Usually, once you've already married the person for their great sex, you then realize that they really had nothing else to offer you; you're incompatible, or even worse, someone ends up physically hurt, behind bars or six feet under.

Many people say sex is one of the most important parts of marriage. How can I marry someone without knowing that very important part of them? I agree that sex is a very important part of marriage. But God knows all including you and everything about you. He knows just what you want and need sexually. If you dare to obey Him and do things

His way, He will not let you down in such an important area of your life, sex, and marriage.

For clarity, I'm not talking about refraining from sex to make a man marry you for sex. That is foolishness and possibly even a form of witchcraft (manipulation). I'm talking about refraining from sex to honor God with your body because you love God and desire to please Him. It's about seeking God regarding your mate and waiting on His approval before marriage. God will honor you he knows what you need sexually; more than you do.

You will not be let down when you have sex in your marriage, if you seek God and wait on him for your marriage. If you are being abstinent until marriage for any other reason and you don't seek God regarding your mate before you get married, then I can't promise you how that's going to work out for you. All I can say is good luck with that. God intended marriage to be a blessing from Him, not a curse. If you wait on God for it, I just can't see Him letting you down. That's just my opinion on this and guarding your body sexually. The Word of God is clear about sex and how to guard your body against it outside of marriage:

> *Nevertheless, to avoid fornication, let every man have his own wife, and let every woman have her own husband.* (1 Corinthians 7:2 KJV)
>
> *Run from sexual sin! No other sin so clearly affects the body as this one does. For sexual immorality is a sin against your own body.* (1 Corinthians 6:18 NLT)
>
> *God's will is for you to be holy, so stay away from all sexual sin.* (1 Thessalonians 4:3 NLT)
>
> *So put to death the sinful, earthly things lurking within you. Have nothing to do with sexual immorality, impurity, lust, and evil desires. Don't be greedy, for a greedy person is an idolater, worshiping the things of this world.* (Colossians 3:5 NLT)

These are just a few things the Bible has to say about guarding your body against sexual sins; I think this is enough for you to get the point. It's unfortunate to say, but I think more people have fallen into sexual sin even as Christians than not. Most like me at one point; I think lacked the understanding of what they were actually doing through this sin (fornicating/adultery). Unfortunately, there aren't many churches teaching holiness; therefore, many Christians just know they are supposed to live holy, but they don't have a clue how to; it's this ignorance that is destroying us.

> *My people are being destroyed for lack of knowledge: because thou hast rejected knowledge, I will also reject thee, that thou shalt be no priest to me: seeing thou hast forgotten the law of thy God, I will also forget thy children.* (Hosea 4:6 KJV)

Like everything else you want to be successful in, refraining from sex until marriage will take discipline. You can't eat all types of unhealthy foods and drinks, never exercise and expect to get a lean, clean, in shape, toned body with a nice six pack. You can't put yourself in compromising positions and expect to be successful in keeping yourself pure until marriage. Remember, "We wrestle not against flesh and blood, but against principalities, against powers, against the rulers of the darkness of this world, against spiritual wickedness in high places" (Ephesians 6:12 KJV). Therefore, you can only expect what you're giving life to (what you're feeding yourself with) to kill what you're not. If you're giving life to (feeding your flesh with) the things you watch, the places you go (ex. strip clubs) and the people you surround yourself with (fornicators who very vocally express their sexual desires and experiences) then you can't expect your spirit to override your flesh. If you want your spirit to override your flesh then you have to feed your spirit (read, study, and meditate on the word of God, fast and pray, fellowship with other believers of Christ, listen to and watch godly music and media, etc. and avoid the opposite) because what you're giving life to will override what you're not giving life to. Feeding your spirit will help you succeed in this area as well as every other area of your life.

You may be saying to yourself; that all sounds good but what about when the person I'm dating and myself are alone. How do we control ourselves when we are physically attracted to each other? Well the first thing I'll say to you is maybe it's not a good idea for you to be alone together until you develop self control. What am I saying? Set boundaries for yourselves according to yourselves. You should be guarding your eyes therefore you shouldn't be watching sexually explicit media individually; and certainly you shouldn't be watching it together to tempt you while you are together. Set boundaries on your conversation; don't talk about sex or things that lead to sex keep your conversation (body language and verbal communication) clear from sex. Yes you are in a relationship and you should be able to talk to each other about anything but in this area you have to be wise. If your partner is having a weak moment and begins expressing his or her sexual desire you need to be able to pray his or her desire away at the moment not join them which will lead to sin.

For some, not kissing may be a boundary. While I don't believe kissing before marriage is a sin, if you know you can't control yourself from going further after kissing then you may want to consider not kissing until marriage. I can't tell you all of the physical steps you need to take to be successful in your celibacy or Holiness journey. You know yourself, so guard yourself properly according to the word of God and ask God for help in this and every area of your life.

God does not hold you accountable for what you don't know. However, now you do know, don't be upset because you will be held accountable for what you know. Remember, it is sin to know what you ought to do and then not do it (James 4:17 NLT). God will help you because He loves you and this is what He requires of you. Why would God require something from you that He hasn't given you the power to achieve? He won't! He will help you if you want to be helped.

> *The temptations in your life are no different from what others experience. And God is faithful. He will not allow the temptation to be more than you can stand. When you are tempted, he will show you a way out so that you can endure.* (1 Corinthians 10:13 NLT)

What makes sex so dangerous outside of marriage or with a person or persons God does not intend for you is the soul tie that you make when doing so. When you have sex with someone your souls are joined. God created sex for marriage to make two individuals one flesh. Every person you have sex with, you become one with in God's eyes and in the spiritual realm. The two are united as one. "And the two will become one flesh So they are no longer two, but one flesh. Therefore what God has joined together, let no one separate". (Mark 10:8-9 NIV). Do you understand why it's so hard at times to let go of a person with whom you have been sexually active? If your relationships do not result in marriage and you go from person to person, you are giving a piece of your soul to each person you sleep with.

> *And so, dear brothers and sisters, I plead with you to give your bodies to God because of all he has done for you. Let them be a living and holy sacrifice the kind he will find acceptable. This is truly the way to worship him.* (Romans 12:1 NLT)

Perhaps, you didn't understand all of this before. But now, although you may still think it's impossible, you realize God requires you to abstain from sex before marriage and be faithful in marriage. You desire to honor God and make your body a living sacrifice unto Him by refraining from sex until you marry the husband or wife God has for you. If so let's pray!

> *Father God, in the name of Jesus, I had no idea of the great sin I was committing against my body and You by having sex with those who are not my husband or wife. I thank You for enlightening me with the understanding of Your purpose for sex, and I ask You to forgive me for operating against Your purpose. Father, I desire to give my body to You as a living and holy sacrifice that You will find pleasing and acceptable in Your sight. I thank You, Lord, that now, I have the knowledge in this area that I needed to understand the importance of this. I'm aware that You will now be holding me accountable for my actions in this area. I ask You, Father, to keep me. In my own strength I can't overcome sexual temptations but by Your Spirit, I can. I thank You, Lord, that for every temptation You make a way of escape. I ask You, Lord, to help me see that way every time that I would take it and conquer sinning against my own body by fornicating and or*

committing adultery. I understand now that You created sex as a special gift for a husband and wife; it is a gift I do want to receive. So Father, prepare me for my husband or wife and prepare my husband or wife for me. Lead us to each other by Your Holy Spirit so we can enjoy Your good and perfect will for us in our marriage. In Jesus' name, I pray. Amen!

Chapter 6

GUARDING YOUR SOUL

Take my yoke upon you, Let me teach you, because I am humble and gentle at heart, and you will find rest for your souls. For my yoke is easy to bear, and the burden I give you is light. (Matthew 11:29-30 NLT)

The Enemy's purpose for attacking your soul is to keep you emotionally unstable and unable to carry out God's purpose for your life. He attacks this part of you to interfere with your will to allow God to have His way in your life. Instead, he desires to make you angry with God, to curse God and His (God's) plans for you so you will follow his (the Enemy's) plan.

There are several things that can be said about the soul and many ways we can look at it. But the one thing I want to focus on for the purpose of guarding your soul in this book is viewing your soul as your will and your emotional state of being – the inner you. This is the deepest part of you, your core; the part that holds the key to your joy and true happiness. The soul is the place created by God where we can feel Him. God created us to have a relationship with Him; He is our original soul mate. When we messed up our relationship with God by worshiping other gods and committing so many evil and wicked acts, He still loved us so much that it was important to Him to rekindle our relationship. We did things that hurt Him so much that it caused

Him to destroy us. Yet, He sent His only Son to die for our redemption and reconciliation.

> *For since our friendship with God was restored by the death of his Son while we were still his enemies, we will certainly be saved through the life of his Son. So now we can rejoice in our wonderful new relationship with God because our Lord Jesus Christ has made us friends of God.* (Romans 5:10-11 NLT)

Why is our relationship with God so important to Him? Because we (humanity) are the only ones God created in His image and likeness. Therefore, although we are not God, we are His children; the only ones of all of His creation made to be like Him and to have a relationship with Him.

That's why when God made everything else, He said it was good but it wasn't until man was created that He said what He made was *very* good.

> *So God created great sea creatures and every living thing that scurries and swarms in the water, and every sort of bird each producing offspring of the same kind. And God saw that it was good.* (Genesis 1:21 NLT)

> *Then God said, "Let us make human beings in our image, to be like us. They will reign over the fish in the sea, the birds in the sky, the livestock, all the wild animals on the earth, and the small animals that scurry along the ground. So God created human beings in his own image. In the image of God he created them; male and female he created them. Then God blessed them and said, "Be fruitful and multiply. Fill the earth and govern it. Reign over the fish in the sea, the birds in the sky, and all the animals that scurry along the ground." Then God said, "Look! I have given you every seed bearing plant throughout the earth and all the fruit trees for your food. And I have given every green plant as food for all the wild animals, the birds in the sky, and the small animals that scurry along the ground everything that has life." And this is what happened. Then God looked over all he had made, and he saw that it was very good! And the evening passed and morning came, marking the sixth day.* (Genesis 1:26-31 NLT)

Our souls are the deepest parts of our beings. We find and develop our intimacy with God there. In turn, we access the ability to be truly intimate with our spouses. Before we become close to God, we only know of Him but when we experience Him for ourselves, we become intimate with Him. The foundation of our relationship with Him is made solid from within our souls. I believe God designed our soul for his dwelling place for two important reasons. The first is because our soul is the deepest part of us therefore; the one who dwells there should be the closest to us; God. Once we allow God his residence in our souls we are in true relationship with him; putting him in his rightful place in our lives; first, we learn how to be intimate and in relationship. Secondly it's to show us the reflection of what our earthly marriage should look like because when two marry they share a dwelling within one another's soul also (intimacy). That is why as I stated in the previous chapter when someone has sex with persons other than his or her husband or wife and creates soul ties not ordained by God, it's dangerous.

Because our souls were created as God's residence first and then the dwelling of our husbands or wives second, it is important to be in a relationship and married to God before you are tied to marrying your husband or wife. Your intimacy with God not only teaches you how to love. It also teaches you commitment, loyalty, unconditional love, and forgiveness. Learning how to be intimate with God is crucial for the foundation of your relationship with Him. However, it's also a training ground for your relationship with your spouse. When you learn about God, how to serve Him and be intimate with Him from your soul, you will learn how to do the same with your husband or wife. Many people are ignorant of the fact that the quality of their relationship with God affects the relationship they have with their spouses, for this reason, a lot of marriages don't work out. Because most people don't marry God first; but make so many other soul ties creating bondages and baggage on the inside; even though they want to love and have a successful marriage, they don't really know how.

Maybe, you were also ignorant to this until now. Are you interested in knowing how to develop intimacy with God? I'm sure you have heard the saying, "worship God in spirit and in truth." What does it mean? You become intimate with God as well as worship Him in spirit and in truth through prayer and worship, which eventually leads you to personal dialog. This is what we in Christianity call quiet time with God or spending time with God. How is intimacy with God developed this way? Prayer is talking to God or communicating with Him. Yes, He already knows everything but when you express yourself to Him (your emotions, feelings, everything on your mind and heart), it's really through such expression and questioning that you find the answers you need from God.

It's almost like a counseling session. Not to compare the two, but I do want you to get the full picture I'm trying to paint for you. People go to counseling for several reasons and no, going to counseling doesn't mean something is wrong with you. Personally, I believe everyone can benefit from counseling. People who go to counseling have issues at hand they want to fix or a situation they want to improve. Most times, the counselor does most of the listening and every now and then, he or she will ask you questions: "How does that make you feel?" "Tell me more about that." It's your answers to those questions that really help guide you to the overall answer you're looking for, which led you to the counselor, to begin with.

God the Father is the Almighty Counselor so any and every time you sit with Him, you are destined to always come out feeling better regardless of your situation; sometimes, you get the answers to your questions if God sees fit to answer you. By releasing what's in your heart to God, you acknowledge your inability to handle the problem yourself. It is His ability you need to fix the situation or to help you within the situation. Acknowledging God's ability will lead you to worship. When you worship God, you are accepting who God is and His capabilities. You put aside your issues to focus on the issue solver, God the Father. When you focus on Him and who He is, you realize that no matter how big your problem appears to be, it is small in comparison with God. Worship praises and exalts God, which makes Him want to move that issue on your behalf, so you can have something else to thank and praise Him for. It's through our intimacy with God that our deepest needs are met. How so? Because during this time, you are in fellowship with the One who knows and has all. Therefore, whatever you need, you will find in the presence of God.

But what happens when we make soul ties that shouldn't be made and when we don't allow God to take residence in our souls? When this happens, we allow so many other people and things (substitute gods/idols) to occupy our souls that we lose ourselves (our identity/relationship with God) in the process. Remember, our souls are our wills and emotions; therefore, if God is to dwell in our souls for us to be intimate with Him but He does not, we must ask ourselves what we are using (substitute/idol) to cope with our emotions. What is taking God's place in our souls?

Are we looking to sex outside of marriage, food, shopping, people, and the like for satisfaction? What are you using to fill the void within you? Only God can fill that void and heal your soul from the ravages of the substitutes you have used. Have you ever wondered how people are able to commit suicide if they lose someone close like a family member, lover or friend? Maybe, they've allowed that person to occupy their souls in a way that God did not intend. But more pertinent is that they haven't allowed God to occupy the space that only He can fill.

> *For what shall it profit a man, if he shall gain the whole world and lose his own soul?* (Mark 8:36 KJV)

The above scripture is basically saying you can gain the whole world, riches, fame and fulfill the lust of your flesh (the substitutes for God) but when you're done, you'll still be empty, incomplete, and unfulfilled. If you seek joy and happiness in your temporary possessions, instead of finding eternal joy in God, you may lose your soul to gain the whole world. Don't get me wrong, there is nothing amiss with having nice things and traveling to beautiful places around the world; by all means, this is what you ought to do – enjoy life. God created all of these things for us to enjoy, but He did not create all of them for us to live for and worship; God is a jealous God.

> *You must worship no other gods, for the Lord, whose very name is Jealous, is a God who is jealous about his relationships with you.* (Exodus 34:14 NLT)

God is to be the center of our joy, which is found and developed deep down within our souls. Why is it so important to guard our souls? If you're anything like me, you don't do anything you don't feel like doing (lol). Your soul includes your will and emotions, the very things that fuel your actions. When you're feeling angry, depressed hurt or generally unwell emotionally, you are not inclined to get up and be positive. You don't feel like doing the things that are necessary at the time because your feelings dictate your actions and responses. This at times can be ungodly. Therefore, we need to guard our souls to avoid being misled and used by the Enemy, which is sometimes known as the inner you.

As humans with emotions, we go through things we wouldn't wish on our worst enemy. God never told us that we wouldn't ever have trials or that we would never have any undesirable experiences in life. In fact, He said that we would. The good thing about it is, He also told us that He overcame the world, and because he lives inside of us, we too can overcome

> *I have told you all this so that you may have peace in me. Here on earth you WILL have many trials and sorrows. But take heart, because I have overcome the world.* (John 16:33 NLT)

This is exciting to know, but I'm sure you're asking how we can overcome our emotions, let alone the world? The Bible tells us to:

> *Give all your worries and cares to God, for he cares about you.*
> (1 Peter 5:7 NLT)

> *Don't worry about anything instead, pray about everything. Tell God what you need, and thank him for all he has done. Then you will experience God's peace, which exceeds anything we can understand. His peace will guard your hearts and minds as you live in Christ Jesus.* (Philippians 4:6-7 NLT)

This is what makes guarding your soul easy. You don't have to carry every worry and care that you have. Cast them on God; He can fix them. With God living in us and having an intimate relationship with us, we can freely and comfortably talk to Him about everything. You can place all your cares on Him. You ought to make God your best friend so you can easily relate to Him as you would your earthly friend. The more comfortable you are with someone, the more authentic you will be with him or her. So when you have a friendship with God, casting your burdens on Him will be easy because you have discovered He is trustworthy. Contrarily, when other things and people replace God in your soul, you can't cast your cares on them because they can't help you. As a result, you will find yourself searching for more and more people and things to solve your problems. Alternatively, you will look for other coping methods in futility.

In the opening scripture it says: "Take my yoke upon you, let me teach you, because I am humble and gentle at heart, and you will find rest for your souls." When you take your problems to God, He will take care of them; you will find rest and peace for your soul. At some point in our lives, we experience turmoil and anxiety; we become restless and confused about situations in our lives. Can you think about an issue that had you all worked up? Think about the first to the last thing that you did or thought about how to fix the issue. I am almost certain that the entire time you were all worked up about your problem, you neither consulted God, talked to Him nor even thought about asking Him to intervene.

However, I'm sure that when you somehow turned the matter over to God, you experienced a change in your life whether you found a solution or not. Maybe, you cried out, "God help me!" or you called someone to pray for you. However it happened, when you released that issue to God, it no longer overwhelmed you and kept you restless. We have all been guilty of this at some point in our lives. But here's the beauty of an intimate relationship with God. God says to cast your cares on Him for He cares for you. Now in casting your cares on Him, you are putting your hope and trust in God to handle it. We know that certainly God can handle it and we give it to Him believing that He will.

Sometimes in His awesomeness, God will not only handle the problem but He will show you how to deal with it yourself through

His wisdom. I'm not talking about you coming up with a bright idea or solution to your problem. I'm talking about a divine revelation that God Himself gives as a solution. So what God will do is not only take care of your cares, but He will give you the strategy to handle that issue and others that may arise from time to time in your life. Isn't God amazing?

Somehow, we always seem to forget that God has given us the privilege to cast our cares on Him and so we complicate our lives with worries and unrest. The point is this: when we face life's challenges God should be the first one we go to, not the last resort. Life has proven many times that it's not until we go to Him that we really find the solution – rest for our souls.

Guarding your emotions is not the same as ignoring them, pretending they don't exist or you're not feeling them. Rather, it's reaching a place where your emotions (how you feel) do not control you. You learn to control your emotions as you yield to the will of God in spite of how you feel. God said to cast your cares on Him for He cares for you, for a reason. He knows we will have cares and that there are things that will happen in our lives to cause us to get emotional. He wants our trust even in the deepest and most vulnerable times of our lives. If we can trust Him in the most hurtful areas, we can trust Him in every other area of our lives.

Jesus had emotions; after all, He came from heaven as a human being to experience life on the earth. He had to deal with emotions, temptations, disappointments, and everything we experience as humans. But He also exemplified how to handle them. Jesus could not have felt good knowing that Judas, one of His disciples would betray Him. To know that the very person whom He taught and ate and drank with would betray Him had to be painful; yet, Jesus loved him and treated him no differently than the other disciples. We face a similar situation when the Holy Spirit reveals through discernment that someone close to us is living foul. You know what I mean. The person is with you for all the wrong reasons. Sometimes, it's to get where you are or what you have. Other times, it's to help you reach the mountaintop so they can push you off and take over. They want to steal from, kill, and destroy you.

But as with Judas, those people in your life are pushing you to your destiny; they help shape and mold you into who God wants you to be. Unknown to them, they are assisting in the actualization of God's intensive purpose for our lives. However, that doesn't mean that being betrayed isn't hurtful – it is. But what did Jesus teach us through Judas' betrayal? Did He say, "Yeah, I know Judas is going to betray Me so let Me kill him before he gets Me killed"? Did He say, "Get this two-faced coward away from Me! Who needs enemies when you have friends like this"? No. Jesus knew that Judas would betray Him. Nevertheless, He treated him the same way. Jesus still loved him, still taught him, and even allowed him to betray Him. Perhaps, Jesus said "Father, thank You for Judas; he's assisting in the fulfillment of your good and perfect purpose for My life."

Am I saying be an idiot; let people walk all over you, misuse and abuse you because you are a Christian? Absolutely not! Jesus didn't allow Judas' betrayal to mess with His emotions and make Him retaliate. Basically, Jesus didn't allow Judas's betrayal or the knowledge of it, to change His character. He kept His godly character intact even when He knew Judas would betray Him. Like Jesus, we have control over our actions. Our emotions will come and go; they will go up, down and around and around like a roller coaster, but we don't have to allow them to toss us about concerning God's will and purpose for us. We don't have to let our emotions cause us to give up on God's purpose for our lives because we're hurting.

We need to be like Jesus and keep our focus on God's purpose for us, not what we are going through at the time. You may say, "I ain't Jesus, and I ain't there yet. If you slap me, I'm going to slap you back!" I have said the same thing and felt this way as well using the excuse that God is still working on me. We are not Jesus, but if we are Christians, we are to be Christlike. Striving to be like Jesus ought to be more of your normal than all of the work that God is still doing on you (lol). We ought to make it our practice to be like Jesus instead of conveniently using the excuse that we aren't there yet. Maybe we aren't there yet because we aren't trying to be; we don't really want to be.

All I'm saying is even our emotions good and bad work together for our good and God's purpose for our lives if we remember that God is in control and has given us the control over our souls (our wills and emotions).

> *And we know that God causes everything to work together for the good of those who love God and are called according to his purpose for them.* (Romans 8:28 NLT).

Maybe you haven't recognized it, but do you know there was a time in the Bible when Jesus described His emotional state?

> *Then Jesus went with them to the olive grove called Gethsemane, and he said, "Sit here while I go over there to pray." He took Peter and Zebedee's two sons, James and John, and he became anguished and distressed. He told them, "My soul is crushed with grief to the point of death. Stay here and keep watch with me." He went on a little farther and bowed with his face to the ground, praying, "My Father! If it is possible, let this cup of suffering be taken away from me. Yet I want your will to be done, not mine."* (Matthew 26:36-39 NLT).

There was another time in the Bible when Jesus actually displayed His emotions. He cried when His friend Lazarus died. He shows us that it's ok and actually good to cry. Sometimes, our emotions will call for that reaction. But what did Jesus do immediately after He cried? He raised Lazarus from the dead allowing God's glory to be revealed. The purpose for Lazarus' death was accomplished; God was glorified. Read John 11:1-45 for a clearer understanding of this account. Below is a brief summary to help you see what I believe was Jesus' frustration; and is what caused Him to get emotional.

Jesus loved Mary, Martha, and Lazarus. Lazarus was sick and his sisters Mary and Martha sent a message to Jesus to let Him know. Jesus responded: "Lazarus' sickness will not end in death. It happened for the glory of God so that the Son of God will receive glory from this." Therefore, unlike what Mary and Martha wanted Jesus to do, Jesus stayed where He was for the next two days; He didn't go to them right away. When Jesus arrived in Bethany, Lazarus had already been in his grave for four days. Martha said to Jesus, "Lord if only you had been here, my brother would not have died." Jesus spoke to Martha and then sent her to get her sister Mary. When Mary came to Jesus, she said the same thing as her sister Martha, "Lord if only you had been here, my brother would not have died."

Scripture says when Jesus saw Mary weeping and the other people wailing, a deep anger welled up within Him and He was deeply troubled. He asked them where they had buried Lazarus. As He walked to the tomb, Jesus wept and was still angry. The people made comments saying: "This man healed a blind man. Couldn't He have kept Lazarus from dying?" I don't think these people's comments were what angered Jesus. What I believe caused His anger and frustration was the fact that He had already told Mary and Martha that Lazarus' sickness was not unto death but for the glory of God. However, because Lazarus had died, they didn't believe what Jesus told them. If they did, they wouldn't have reacted to his death as if it was the end.

Jesus told them his sickness was not unto death but for the glory of God. What does that statement say in itself? It says that Lazarus' death had to happen but it was not for death; it was for a resurrection, which would reveal the glory of God. Could that be why it seems like things get worse before they get better? Could it be that something has to die before life can really happen? But because of what Jesus told them, they should have known, Lazarus' death was not the end; God's glory would be and for that reason alone, they should not have responded as they did.

How should they have reacted? I mean, their brother did die! It may sound crazy but because of what Jesus already told them, they should have been excited about their brother's death. His death should have made them realize although they may not have known how, God's glory was going to follow Lazarus' death!

Sometimes, we become emotional because we believe in something that God has shown us but those around us just don't get it. Because we see clearly (through our faith) as if the thing is right there and others just can't see it, we get frustrated like Jesus did in this case. At times, the situation can even cause us to be emotional wrecks. But we should not allow frustration to cause us to forget our purpose or goals. We must bounce back from the frustration or emotional disappointment and carry out God's intended purpose in the situation for God's glory to be manifested. What am I saying? "Don't let your frustration terminate your assignment!"

I've noticed when you're just living life from day to day, not trying to accomplish a task God has given you your world seems great. Every day is sunshine; everything seems to go well for you. You feel on top of the world; you are just in such a state of peace. But as soon as you begin to work toward the very thing that God has called you to, your whole world turns upside down. Everything around you turns into disarray. The Enemy's purpose for all of this chaos is to get you to such a low emotional state that you will not press forward to accomplish the task God has given you. He sends these things your way to deter you from being willing to do what you know you're supposed to be doing because it's difficult at the time. He wants you to settle for what appears to be less complicated.

As I stated earlier in this book, God made many promises to me when I was a little girl; most of which I am still waiting for. Don't you think the Enemy brought every promise back to my memory during the process of writing this book? Of course! Not to remind me of how great the promises are or of the goodness of Jesus, but simply to make me focus on the fact that I still do not physically possess those promises yet. He did this all in an attempt to make me doubt God, get angry with Him and not write this book to encourage God's people. I must admit that as I wrote, my mind wandered to everything I could think about to keep me distracted from the task God put before me. I will also admit that some days, it looked like the Enemy had won. Some days, I didn't feel like writing, praying, reading God's Word or doing anything that I should have been doing. Those were the days when I paid too much attention to the chaos around me while waiting on the promises of God to be fulfilled in my life that seemed as if they would never happen.

I was an emotional wreck. Sometimes, my emotional state stopped me from writing. There were days I cried and I knew why but other times, I couldn't explain my tears if you paid me. But through it all,

God's purpose for me may have been delayed, but it certainly was not denied. For by God's grace and mercy, I received the strength to persevere and press forward. Through me, God completed the task He set. Did you learn anything from this book thus far? Has it encouraged you in at least one area of your life? Did it bless you in any way, shape, form, or fashion? If so, then imagine if I had allowed my emotional state to keep me from producing it. You would not have been blessed through it, and God would not have gotten the glory out of it.

I wonder what word God has already spoken over you that like Mary, Martha, and me seems contrary to your current reality. Have you forgotten the victorious end (the word God spoke to you) that Jesus already pronounced over you? What are you going through right now, that has you in emotional turmoil, which has been placed there by God, not unto death (to kill you) but for His glory? Can't think of anything? Let me help you!

> *"For I know the plans I have for you," says the Lord. "They are plans for good and not for disaster, to give you a future and a hope.* (Jeremiah 29:11 NLT)

Your troubles, heartaches, pains, and disappointments are only present to lead you to God's glory in your life. Stop your weeping; get off the emotional train wreck and allow God's glory to be revealed in your life. After all, this is what you were created for – God's glory! Just imagine if Jesus had not walked to Lazarus' grave even in His emotional state and allowed God's glory to be revealed. Lazarus would have been in His grave from that day until now.

Guarding your soul is not allowing your circumstances or emotions to keep you from doing what the Lord desires of you. It is letting God fulfill His purpose in your life. Remember that the Enemy's purpose for messing with your emotions and causing tribulations and trials is to destroy you, make you lose faith and give up on life and God. But God uses your emotions, test, and trials to make you strong.

> *Dear brothers and sisters, when troubles of any kind come your way, consider it an opportunity for great joy. For you know that when your faith*

is tested, your endurance has a chance to grow. So let it grow, for when your endurance is fully developed, you will be perfect and complete, needing nothing. (James 1:2-4 NLT)

Don't let your emotions, the disappointments, and hard times that you go through change your will to live for God. Rather, make living for God change and control your emotions so you are led by God in your actions and desires no matter what emotional state you are in.

Then Jesus said to his disciples, "If any of you wants to be my follower, you must turn from your selfish ways, take up your cross, and follow me. If you try to hang on to your life, you will lose it. But if you give up your life for my sake, you will save it. And what do you benefit if you gain the whole world but lose your own soul? Is anything worth more than your soul? (Matthew 16:24-26 NLT)

Now that we understand the importance of guarding our souls, let's pray for our souls!

Father God, in the name of Jesus, I thank You for this enlightenment of Your purpose for creating my soul. I realize that only humans have souls because we were the only creation made for intimacy with You. Forgive me for all of the soul ties I made in ignorance and knowingly in place of You. Now that I'm aware of Your purpose for my soul, I desire to be made whole in the deepest part of me – my soul. I desire to be intimate with You Lord, to know You in spirit and in truth and to develop that foundation where You take residence in my soul. I don't ever want to replace You with anything or anyone else again. I realize that this is impossible anyway; You can't be replaced. I evict any and every substitute god that has taken residence in my soul right now, in the name of Jesus. And I replace it with You Father God! Come, reside in me. Make my soul Your dwelling place. You are welcome here, now and forever. In Jesus' name, I pray. Amen!

Chapter 7

GUARDING YOUR SPIRIT

> *Those who live only to satisfy their own sinful nature will harvest decay and death from that sinful nature. But those who live to please the Spirit will harvest everlasting life from the Spirit.* (Galatians 6:8 NLT)

The Enemy's purpose for attacking your spirit is to prevent you from being controlled by the Holy Spirit, which leads to life, and to cause you to be controlled by the Enemy through his evil spirits, which leads to death.

What is the spirit, and how do we live to please it? The word "spirit" is translated from the Hebrew word *ru'ach* and the Greek word *pneu'ma*. These words refer to God's active force, the Holy Spirit, God. In this world, there are many spirits, all of which derive from God the Father (the spirit of light) or from the Enemy (the spirit of darkness). Make no mistake about it, when I speak about guarding your spirit, I am certainly not speaking about protecting anything evil from the spirit of darkness. I am speaking about shielding the most precious gift God has given you once you've received His Son Jesus Christ as your Lord and Savior – the Holy Spirit. The Holy Spirit is God living inside of you; God's active force living inside of you.

> *Know ye not that ye are the temple of God, and that the Spirit of God dwelleth in you?* (1 Corinthians 3:16 KJV)

Therefore when I speak about guarding the Holy Spirit I'm speaking about guarding; God's active force within you. Isn't God all-powerful? If He is then why does His Spirit need to be guarded? Can't He just overpower every other spirit? Yes, God is all powerful and He can overpower every spirit of darkness. But the main focus, as stated earlier is on guarding the Holy Spirit within you. He will not work actively in your life without your permission just as the spirit of darkness can't work in you unless you allow it to. You may not be aware of when or how you give the spirit of darkness permission to work in you. I'll be talking about all of that in this chapter.

> *All who declare that Jesus is the Son of God have God living in them, and they live in God.* (1 John 4:15 NLT)

> *And God has given us his Spirit as proof that we live in him and he in us.* (1 John 4:13 NLT)

Many believers have different views about the Holy Spirit; and when one receives him. This is understandable because every believer's experience of receiving the Holy Spirit is different.

> *Let me ask you this one question: Did you receive the Holy Spirit by obeying the law of Moses? Of course not! You received the Spirit because you believed the message you heard about Christ.* (Galatians 3:2 NLT)

> *"Did you receive the Holy Spirit when you believed?" he asked them. "No," they replied, "we haven't even heard that there is a Holy Spirit." "Then what baptism did you experience?" he asked. And they replied, "The baptism of John." Paul said, "John's baptism called for repentance from sin. But John himself told the people to believe in the one who would come later, meaning Jesus." As soon as they heard this, they were baptized in the name of the Lord Jesus. Then when Paul laid his hands on them, the Holy Spirit came on them, and they spoke in other tongues and prophesied.* (Acts 19:2-6 NLT)

As seen in the above scripture the Holy Spirit can be received by the laying on of hands. However, for those of you who have not received the Holy Spirit this way and desire the Holy Spirit; as well as those who have received Jesus Christ as your Lord and Savior but aren't sure if you have the Holy Spirit, let me help you.

> *Peter replied, "Each of you must repent of your sins and turn to God, and be baptized in the name of Jesus Christ for the forgiveness of your sins. Then you will receive the gift of the Holy Spirit.* (Acts 2:38 NLT)
>
> *If you love me, obey my commandments. And I will ask the Father, and he will give you another Advocate, who will never leave you. He is the Holy Spirit, who leads into all truth. The world cannot receive him, because it isn't looking for him and doesn't recognize him. But you know him, because he lives with you now and later will be in you.* (John 14:15-17 NLT)
>
> *So if you sinful people know how to give good gifts to your children, how much more will your heavenly Father give the Holy Spirit to those who ask him."* (Luke 11:13 NLT)

Therefore, don't allow yourself to be confused or mislead about the Holy Spirit. If you want to be sure you receive the Holy Spirit repent of your sins and accept Jesus Christ as your Lord and Savior, get baptized, love God and obey his commandments, ask God to fill you with the Holy Spirit, then simply receive the gift of the Holy Spirit as he's given to you.

> *But you will receive power when the Holy Spirit comes upon you. And you will be my witnesses, telling people about me everywhere in Jerusalem, throughout Judea, in Samaria, and to the ends of the earth."* (Acts 1:8 NLT)

It's so important that you receive the Holy Spirit and allow Him to dwell, move, and live freely in and through you.

I believe more than anything that it's the manifestation of the Holy Spirit that confuses believers about whether or not they have the Holy Spirit. If you have accepted Jesus Christ as your Lord and Savior; however, you are not living your life in the way that will allow the Holy Spirit to manifest Himself, more than likely He won't. When you allow the Holy Spirit to manifest Himself then He will do so at the proper time he sees fit. He calls the shots as to when and how that will be.

The "how" is the other source of confusion about the Holy Spirit. The Holy Spirit manifests Himself in more ways than just speaking in tongues. When you sing under the anointing, preach under the anointing and do anything with the power and authority that comes from God, it is not you but the operation of the Holy Spirit inside of you. However, He may not have manifested Himself until you aligned yourself with Him to allow Him to.

Though some Christians are filled with the Holy Spirit immediately upon their salvation I think many Christians don't live out the power of the Holy Spirit because they're waiting on the Holy Spirit to "hit" them before they align themselves with Him (meaning living their lives pleasing to the Lord denying their flesh). They don't realize that aligning themselves with the Holy Spirit enables and activates His continual manifesting power.

Therefore, I believe your acceptance of Jesus Christ as your Lord and Savior is His invitation to come into your heart. However, you must learn how to activate the Holy Spirit by asking God to fill you with the Holy Spirit and submitting your life to God allowing Him to use you, instead of giving that permission to the spirit of darkness that used you before you came to Christ. How does the spirit of darkness use you? Before I explain, take a look at the scriptures below:

> *Take no part in the worthless deeds of evil and darkness; instead expose them. It is shameful even to talk about the things that ungodly people do in secret. But their evil intentions will be exposed when the light shines on them.* (Ephesians 5:11-13 NLT)

> *Their minds are full of darkness; they wander far from the life God gives because they have closed their minds and hardened their hearts against him. They have no sense of Shame. They live for lustful pleasure and eagerly practice every kind of impurity.* (Ephesians 4:18-19 NLT)

> *Because we belong to the day, we must live decent lives for all to see. Don't participate in the darkness of wild parties and drunkenness, or in sexual promiscuity and immoral living, or in quarreling and jealousy. Instead, clothe yourself with the presence of the Lord Jesus Christ. And don't let yourself think about ways to indulge your evil desires.* (Romans 13:13-14 NLT)

You give the spirit of darkness the ability or permission to use and control you by accepting or rejecting Christ, the Spirit of Light. The spirit of darkness and the Spirit of Light work against each other. As the above scriptures say, those under the spirit of darkness wander far from the life God gives. And those used by the Spirit of Light expose the spirit of darkness. You give either spirit the permission to use you by choosing which spirit you want to live by. When you accept Christ, you choose the Spirit of Light. On the other hand, when you reject Christ, you choose the spirit of darkness. Whether you realize it or not, you are welcoming the spirit of darkness into your life by refusing to submit your life to Christ, the Spirit of Light. Thus, you open yourself to the spirit of darkness and fulfilling the lust of the flesh.

Understand that submitting your life to God and allowing Him to use you will be a struggle especially at the beginning of your salvation. When you begin to activate the Holy Spirit within you, the things of the spirit of darkness must leave so that the things of the Holy Spirit can be activated to please God and allow Him to live freely in you for His glory.

In this context, the word "activate" simply means to allow. It is more complicated than it sounds because allowing the Holy Spirit to take over you requires that you disempower your flesh. In other words, you prevent it from having power, authority, and influence over you. This is the complicated part. Remember what I said in the previous chapter about making the Holy Spirit comfortable as He lives inside of you.

> *Those who are dominated by the sinful nature think about sinful things, but those who are controlled by the Holy Spirit think about things that please the Spirit. So letting your sinful nature control your mind leads to death. But letting the Spirit control your mind leads to life and peace. For the sinful nature is always hostile to God. It never did obey God's laws, and it never will. That's why those who are still under the control of their sinful nature can never please God.* (Romans 8:5-8 NLT)

You must learn to activate the Holy Spirit living inside of you because the Holy Spirit's purpose is to empower you to defeat the Enemy for the glory of God. But how can you defeat the Enemy if you are partnering up with him and allowing him to use you instead of allowing God to use you? God is more powerful than the Enemy and every eye will see that at the end of this world; I will provide you with two scriptures to prove it but please don't stop at those two scriptures. Read the Bible in its entirety and pray for understanding and revelation for clarity on anything that you don't fully understand.

Chapter 8

THE DEFEAT OF SATAN

When the thousand years come to an end, satan will be let out of his prison. He will go out to deceive the nations called Gog and Magog in every corner of the earth. He will gather them together for battle a mighty army, as numberless as sand along the seashore. And I saw them as they went up on the broad plain of the earth and surrounded God's people and the beloved city. But fire from heaven came down on the attacking armies and consumed them. Then the devil, who had deceived them, was thrown into the fiery lake of burning sulfur, joining the beast and the false prophet. There they will be tormented day and night forever and ever. (Revelation 20:7-10 NLT)

Jesus replied, "The Son of Man is the farmer who plants the good seed. The field is the world, and the good seed represents the people of the Kingdom. The weeds are the people who belong to the evil one. The enemy who planted the weeds among the wheat is the devil. The harvest is the end of the world, and the harvesters are the angels. Just as the weeds are sorted out and burned in the fire, so it will be at the end of the world. The Son of Man will send his angels, and they will remove from his Kingdom everything that causes sin and all who do evil. And the angels will throw them into the fiery furnace, where there will be weeping and gnashing of teeth. Then the righteous will shine like the sun in their Father's Kingdom. Anyone with ears to hear should listen and understand! (Matthew 13:37-43 NLT)

If you want to live a victorious Christian life here on earth, you have to allow the Holy Spirit within you to be activated and show that He's more powerful than the Enemy in your life.

So how do you do that? As scripture states "those who live to please the Spirit will harvest everlasting life from the Spirit." So the question is how do you please the Holy Spirit? Before we talk about how to please the Holy Spirit, let's talk about some things that displease the Holy Spirit.

> *And do not bring sorrow to God's Holy Spirit by the way you live. Remember, he has identified you as his own, guaranteeing that you will be saved on the day of redemption. Get rid of all bitterness, rage, anger, harsh words, and slander, as well as all types of evil behavior.* (Ephesians 4:30-31 NLT)

The very first words of the preceding verse tell how to displease the Holy Spirit: "Do not bring sorrow to God's Holy Spirit by the way you live." This means that you can displease the Holy Spirit by your lifestyle. In case you don't know what kind of lifestyle is displeasing to God, the next part of the scripture describes it for you. Don't you just love the Lord and His clarity? "Get rid of all bitterness, rage, anger, harsh words, and slander, as well as all types of evil behavior." I can hear you saying, again, "Well, that's just impossible; I'm only human. I have feelings and living in this evil world, things happen to me, bad things. I can't help that they affect me and sometimes they cause these evil things and behaviors to come out of me. I'm sorry; I just can't help it."

Please, do not forget the last chapter on guarding your soul (will and emotions). God knows all of what you've been through, and He wants you to bring all of it to Him. He will show you how to overcome and take control of your emotions and situations by the Holy Spirit lest they control you. What happens when you are out of control, displeasing the Holy Spirit but pleasing your flesh? You will harvest decay and death from that sinful nature.

You don't have to be spiritual to know and understand the concept of reaping what you sow. It is true in both good and evil. It does not take rocket science to know if you live your life only to please your flesh, you will reap accordingly. First of all, pleasing the flesh means you have no self-control, which inevitably leads to disaster. How so you ask? Humans are the most difficult of all God's creations to satisfy. We tend to want what we want, when we want it and that seems to be everything we see when we see it. If you have no self-control, and you want something, you are willing to do anything and hurt anybody in the process. That's why the scripture says that those who live only to satisfy their own sinful nature will harvest decay and death from that sinful nature. The process of fulfilling that sinful nature will kill you, and sometimes, it can kill others physically, mentally, spiritually, or emotionally.

Why does the Bible tell us to be filled with the Holy Spirit and not our flesh? Because our flesh has strong desires, which nine times out of ten are not good for us. Thus, if we're led by our flesh, it will lead us to things that are not good for us. But the all-knowing Holy Spirit not only knows but wants what's best for us. Look at this scripture:

> *Don't be drunk with wine, because that will ruin your life. Instead, be filled with the Holy Spirit, singing psalms and hymns and spiritual songs among yourselves, and making music to the Lord in your hearts. And give thanks for everything to God the Father in the name of our Lord Jesus Christ.* (Ephesians 5:18-20 NLT)

It is fair to conclude that if you can displease the Holy Spirit by the way you live then you can please the Holy Spirit by the way you live. Remember the Holy Spirit is living in you so it makes sense that your lifestyle will determine if you are pleasing Him or not. How do you live to please the Holy Spirit? The above scripture tells us this also.

Let's be honest, in this life when you are going through something difficult, I mean really going through a hard time, it's much easier to do what your flesh tells you to do than to handle it the way God says. Why not drink, smoke, have sex or even fight your problems away (the quick fix). The Word of God is our blueprint for living and it has a lot to say about life. It tells us, "Be filled with the Holy Spirit, singing psalms and hymns, and spiritual songs among yourselves, and making music to the Lord in your hearts. And give thanks for everything to God the Father in the name of our Lord Jesus Christ."

Who in their right minds when they're going through something difficult or hurtful wants to sing psalms and hymns and make music to the Lord in their hearts? And certainly, only a crazy person would be thankful for hard times. Is that what you are saying? As I stated in the last chapter, God is trying to teach us how to cast our cares on Him, not on ourselves, others or our flesh. How can casting your cares on God please Him? How does it make Him happy? He is pleased with your faith, obedience and trust in Him.

When you release your problems and concerns to God, you are in effect saying, "Here is this thing that is dear to me. I may have a way that I see fit to handle it but I'm giving it to You because I trust that You know the best way to deal with it." We need faith to please God, but I don't think we realize how much our ability to trust God affects our faith in Him. I believe faith and trust go hand in hand. Therefore, when you cast your cares on God displaying your trust in Him, you please Him; It is an act of faith. Yes, there is much more to pleasing God, and I believe the below scripture will help you understand what it takes:

> *Finally, dear brothers and sisters, we urge you in the name of the Lord Jesus to live in a way that pleases God, as we have taught you. You live this way already, and we encourage you to do so even more. For you remember what we taught you by the authority of the Lord Jesus. God's will is for you to be holy, so stay away from all sexual sin. Then each of you will control his own body and live in holiness and honor not in lustful passion like the pagans who do not know God and his ways. Never harm or cheat a fellow believer in this matter by violating his wife, for the Lord avenges all such sins, as we have solemnly warned you before. God has called us to live holy lives, not impure lives. Therefore, anyone who refuses to live by these rules is not disobeying human teaching but is rejecting God, who gives his Holy Spirit to you.* (1 Thessalonians 4:1-8 NLT)

If we don't learn to be filled with the Holy Spirit instead of our flesh, it will lead us to decay and death as the Bible says. I think you can now understand how. However, just in case you still don't understand why it's so important to guard your spirit; let me try one last time to help you. Let me remind you once again of this scripture:

> *For we are not fighting against flesh-and-blood enemies, but against evil rulers and authorities of the unseen world, against mighty powers in this dark world and against evil spirits in the heavenly places. Therefore, put on every piece of God's armor so you will be able to resist the enemy in the time of evil. Then after the battle you will still be standing firm.* (Ephesians 6:12-13 NLT)

You see this thing is bigger than you fighting your temptations and flesh. If you can't win the fight against yourself and your flesh, certainly, it will be even more difficult for you to fight against the evil powers of the Enemy. I have good news for you who are in Christ Jesus but before I give you that good news, I feel the need for us to pray again:

> *Father God, in the name of Jesus, I come to You right now surrendering to Your Holy Spirit. Father, I recognize Your Holy Spirit as God, and I invite You into my heart. Father God, cleanse and purge me from any and every unclean spirit that I have entertained and allowed in my life to control me. I now invite Your Holy Spirit to take full control over me, my mind, my heart, my body, my soul, and my spirit; help me Lord to guard my spirit from this day forth. Live in me God and use me by Your spirit to be a light in this dark world to live the life You created me to live. In Jesus' name, I pray and thank You, Lord. Amen!*

The Good News

> *The Spirit of God, who raised Jesus from the dead, lives in you. And just as God raised Jesus from the dead, he will give life to your mortal bodies by this same Spirit living within you. Therefore, dear brothers and sisters, you have no obligation to do what your sinful nature urges you to do. For if you live by its dictates, you will die. But if through the power of the Spirit you put to death the deeds of your sinful nature, you will live. For all who are led by the Spirit of God are children of God. So you have not received a Spirit that makes you fearful slaves. Instead, you received*

God's Spirit when he adopted you as his own children. Now we call him "Abba, Father." For his spirit joins our spirit to affirm that we are God's children. (Romans 8:11-16 NLT)

AND PRAISE GOES RIGHT HERE!!!!!!

Therefore, guard your spirit. Once you've received Jesus Christ as your Lord and Savior, you have the power to do so!

Chapter 9

BE YE HOLY FOR GOD IS HOLY

The Enemy's purpose for trying to keep you from living holy is to keep you from living out who you were created to be. He wants to hinder you from living out and carrying out your life as God the Father intended in power, love, with a sound mind, and the fullness and abundance of joy. The Enemy attacks you to keep you from living holy so that you won't know who, whose, and what you really are. So that you will not hear or understand God clearly concerning your life and the lives of others. More importantly, he attacks you to keep you from living holy and exercising the power and authority over Him that you really possess. His plan is to steal your success, prosperity, and the abundant life God wants you to have.

> *Even before he made the world, God loved us and chose us in Christ to be holy and without fault in his eyes. God decided in advance to adopt us into his own family by bringing us to himself through Jesus Christ. This is what he wanted to do, and it gave him great pleasure.* (Ephesians 1:4-5 NLT)

> *And I give myself as a holy sacrifice for them so they can be made holy by your truth.* (John 17:19 NLT)

> *For God saved us and called us to live a holy life. He did this, not because we deserved it, but because that was his plan from before the beginning of time to show us his grace through Christ Jesus.* (2 Timothy 1:9 NLT)

So you must live as God's obedient children. Don't slip back into your old ways of living to satisfy your own desires. You didn't know any better then. But now you must be holy in everything you do, just as God who chose you is holy. For the Scriptures say, "You must be holy because I am holy." And remember that the heavenly Father to whom you pray has no favorites. He will judge or reward you according to what you do. So you must live in reverent fear of him during your time here as "TEMPORARY RESIDENTS." For you know that God paid a ransom to save you from the empty life you inherited from your ancestors. And it was not paid with mere gold or silver, which lose their value. It was the precious blood of Christ, the sinless, spotless Lamb of God. God chose him as your ransom long before the world began, but now in these last days he has been revealed for your sake. Through Christ you have come to trust in God. And you have placed your faith and hope in God because he raised Christ from the dead and gave him great glory. You were cleansed from your sins when you obeyed the truth, so now you must show sincere love to each other as brothers and sisters. Love each other deeply with all your heart. For you have been born again, but not to a life that will quickly end. Your new life will last forever because it comes from the eternal, living word of God. (1 Peter 1:14-23 NLT emphasis added)

God's purpose for us to live holy lives is not to make us miserable and miss out on all of the fun in life, this lie however, is what the Enemy wants us to think. But God's purpose for us to live Holy is actually the complete opposite; to make us truly live.

The thief's purpose is to steal and kill and destroy. My purpose is to give them a rich and satisfying life. (John 10:10 NLT)

God is calling us to holiness. Why? Because He made us in His image, and He is holy. In essence, He is simply calling us back to Him. Don't let the Enemy trick you with a carnal mindset like he did with Eve in the garden of Eden. Look at how crafty he is, yet, not so intelligent. Perhaps, we are the ones who are not so intelligent when we fall for his lies because they are so stupid. Examine Eve and Satan's encounter and notice how foolishly Eve was deceived:

> *The Lord God placed the man in the Garden of Eden to tend and watch over it. But the Lord God warned him, "You may freely eat the fruit of every tree in the garden except the tree of the knowledge of good and evil. If you eat its fruit, you are sure to die."* (Genesis 2:15-17 NLT)

> *The serpent was the shrewdest of all the wild animals the Lord God had made. One day he asked the woman, "Did God really say you must not eat the fruit from any of the trees in the garden?" "Of course we may eat fruit from the trees in the garden," the woman replied. "It's only the fruit from the tree in the middle of the garden that we are not allowed to eat. God said, You must not eat it or even touch it; if you do you will die." "You won't die! The serpent replied to the woman. "God knows that your eyes will be opened as soon as you eat it, and you will be like God, knowing both good and evil."* (Genesis 3:1-5 NLT)

"You won't die!" the serpent replied to the woman. "God knows that your eyes will be opened as soon as you eat it, and you will be like God, knowing both good and evil."

The Enemy tricked Eve into doing something (eating the forbidden fruit) to get something that she already had. God created us in His image and likeness. Therefore, she didn't have to eat a fruit to be like God; she was already like God because He created her to be. I wonder what lies the Enemy has told you in your life to lead you to sell your soul, integrity, morals, beliefs, and character in exchange for what's already yours. What the Enemy really did with Eve was lead her away from the very thing that he was tempting her to go the wrong way for. He uses the same tactics on us when we fall for his lies. In Eve's case, it was the image and likeness of God. For you, it may be your wealth, prosperity, relationships or anything he can use to deter you from doing what God said.

If you've gotten anything from this book, I pray it's the importance of being holy on your Christian journey. God says be ye holy for I am holy; I'm sure you all understand now that it's through holiness that you discover the truth. It's because of this truth that you encounter and possess the blessings of God! For example, if you are living holy and you desire a spouse, not just any spouse but your God-ordained spouse, it's through living holy that you will receive him or her.

> *Then the lord God said, "It is not good for the man to be alone. I will make a helper who is just right for him."* (Genesis 2:18 NLT)

The Lord already has this God-ordained spouse for you and as I said, it's through living holy that you will get the person. But here's how the Enemy will trick you right away from receiving what's already yours; and into the lie that his way is the way to get you what you want; just like he did Eve. You may be living holy waiting on your God-ordained spouse when the Devil intervenes telling you, "You've been waiting forever; look at everyone else getting married. They didn't live holy before doing so. You're going about it the wrong way. If you want to get married, you have to show the individual you want to marry just what he or she will be getting in the marriage."

In other words, you have to persuade them to marry you by having sex. You have to put it down in the bedroom and show them what they will be missing if they don't marry you. We know this is not the way of God, and we covered why in the previous chapter. However, for a brief recap, we know that with sex off of the table, we can see the person for who he or she really is; our vision is clearer, not blinded by the sex. Also, this way, we can see whether or not we are compatible, if we can communicate, and discuss what we desire in our future as husband and wife.

Living God's way, and of course, through prayer and seeking, God will lead us to our God- ordained spouses. However, if we listen to Satan when he tells us to forget about God's way because it's taking too long and it's not working, we end up giving the best of ourselves to the wrong person. Consequently, we are left hurt and feeling worthless because we gave up our best and that still wasn't good enough; for the person that wasn't God-ordained for us. You end up not getting the spouse or getting the wrong spouse and being led away from the actual promise of God. Whereas, if you lived holy, eventually, in God's appointed time, you would have gotten the God-ordained spouse God had for you, to begin with.

The Enemy tricks us by causing us to believe it's impossible to live holy as God requires. He leads you to believe it's easier and more exciting not to. Sure, it may be a struggle or challenge at first to live holy, but by the grace of God and the power of His Holy Spirit, you can do it! You just have to be willing. One of the biggest lies the Enemy tells Christians about living holy is that you have to be anointed or called. That's not true! To live holy, you simply have to make the choice. When you make that choice from your heart and seek the Lord's help in this area, by the help of the Holy Spirit you will live holy.

Anything of real value or substance is worth working for. Most times, working for it is not easy but because it's not easy doesn't mean it's not possible or that it's just not God's will for you. You won't say, "Well, if God wanted me to earn a degree, He wouldn't make college so difficult." Or, "If college was in God's will for me, I wouldn't be struggling so hard; it wouldn't be so difficult for me." The reality is while you are in college, you will face difficult times, no matter how smart you are. You will become overwhelmed and challenged. However, that doesn't mean that God didn't call you to college or it's not His will for you to get your degree. You have to work hard for that accomplishment; it will be worth it.

It's the same with holiness; it may seem difficult at first because you are denying your flesh but if you work at it with the help of the Holy Spirit you can be holy. More than that degree, it will be worth working for. I'm not saying you ought to work at holiness like a duty; I'm just using this as an example. What I'm saying is if you love God, your desire should be to please Him. In doing so, you will willingly rid your life of all the things that aren't pleasing to Him; even if you have to work hard at it every day.

> *Jesus replied, "You must love the Lord your God with all your heart, all your soul, and all your mind." This is the first and greatest commandment.* (Matthew 22:37-38 NLT)

Therefore, if you love God with all of your heart, all your soul, and all your mind, you should do whatever is necessary to please Him. And remember, you please God by the way you live. At this point, I'm sure you know that way is to live holy.

Maybe, some of you are thinking, "Why can't I just be a good person, mind my business and not hurt anybody?" "Why can't that just be enough to satisfy God?" "Why do I have to live holy?" We are God's children; we are to look like, live like, and reflect God throughout the earth. Jesus wasn't just a good person; He didn't just mind His business and not hurt anyone. Jesus cared about us and loved us so much that He died for us. He feeds, protects, loves, and provides for us, and even His enemies unconditionally. He asks of us as His children, to do the same. Clearly, God tells us to be holy because He is holy and He is our Father. We cannot overcome the world if we are like it or less than it.

> *You have heard the law that says, "Love your neighbor" and hate your enemy. But I say, love your enemies! Pray for those who persecute you! In that way, you will be acting as true children of your Father in heaven. For he gives his sunlight to both the evil and the good, and he sends rain on the just and the unjust alike. If you love only those who love you, what reward is there for that? Even corrupt tax collectors do that much. If you are kind only to your friends, how are you different from anyone else? Even pagans do that. But you are to be perfect, even as your Father in heaven is perfect.* (Matthew 5:43-48 NLT)

> *I tell you the truth, anyone who believes in me will do the same works I have done, and even greater works, because I am going to be with the Father.* (John 14:12 NLT)

> *Feed the hungry, and help those in trouble. Then your light will shine out from the darkness, and the darkness around you will be as bright as noon.* (Isaiah 58:10 NLT)

> *Give justice to the poor and the orphan; uphold the rights of the oppressed and the destitute.* (Psalms 82:3 NLT)

> *Give generously to the poor, not grudgingly, for the Lord your God will bless you in everything you do.* (Deuteronomy 15:10 NLT)

> *Make allowance for each other's faults, and forgive anyone who offends you. Remember, the Lord forgave you, so you must forgive others.* (Colossians 3:13 NLT)

> *If the world hates you, remember that it hated me first. The world would love you as one of its own if you belonged to it, but you are no longer part of the world. I chose you to come out of the world, so it hates you.* (John 15:18-19 NLT)

We should not expect the world (those in the darkness) to like or agree with us. If they oppose us then that says we must not think like, act like, and live like the world. It does not mean we think we are better than them but it is through our different lifestyles, attitudes, and behaviors they will see Jesus. Something that helps me daily on my Christian journey, especially in my interactions with non-believers is the fact that for some, my life is the only Bible they're reading; and I add on to that; until they accept Jesus Christ as their Lord and Savior because of my proper representation of Christ! It is not always easy to walk this Christian walk and live holy in a world full of evil and darkness but what the Word of God tells us and what I pray you've gotten from this book is that it is doable, and more than worth it.

God has given us everything we need to live holy lives. He gave His Son Jesus' life for us and gave us the gift of the Holy Spirit to fulfill our mission on the earth and live holy doing so. Will people laugh at you, look at you funny, call you names and all other kinds of foolishness for living holy? Sure, they will. But remember, they did the same thing to Jesus Christ. If you call yourself a Christian that means that you are Christlike.

> *The leading priests and teachers of religious law also MOCKED JESUS. "He saved others," they scoffed, "but he can't save himself!* (Mark 15:31 NLT)

> *When they arrived at the house, Jesus wouldn't let anyone go in with him except Peter, John, James, and the little girl's father and mother. The house was filled with people weeping and wailing, but he said, "Stop the weeping! She isn't dead; she's only asleep." BUT THE CROWD LAUGHED AT HIM because they all knew she had died. Then Jesus took her by the hand*

and said in a loud voice, "My child, get up! And at that moment her life returned, and she immediately stood up! Then Jesus told them to give her something to eat. (Luke 8:51-55 NLT)

Because you are Christlike, you will suffer some things as Christ did. However, you will not suffer in vain. If you suffer for Christ, you will also share His glory.

And since we are his children, we are his heirs. In fact, together with Christ we are heirs of God's glory. But if we are to share his glory, we must also share his suffering. (Romans 8:17 NLT)

Be encouraged. God is with and for you; therefore, who can be against you?

What shall we then say to these things? If God be for us, who can be against us? (Romans 8:31 KJV)

When you look at the life of Jesus, Moses, Noah and all the other great people in the Bible, you will discover; they were not always treated kindly. But that didn't stop them from being who God called them to be or from fulfilling God's purpose in and through their lives; you shouldn't stop either. If you study the lives of these great people, I'm sure you'll find times in their lives when it would have been easier for them to live like everyone else. There were times when not being so close to God and sensitive to His desires being fulfilled above theirs on the earth may have seemed easier to do. But not once will you find that they gave into those times, and if they did, certainly, they repented and got right back on track with God's plan. God's purpose was fulfilled through them. For that reason, we are privileged to read and study about them, encouraged and guided by their lives.

Nothing about your life was designed by mistake. God does not make mistakes. No matter how good or bad they were or whether or not you grew up with them in your life, you were born to the right parents. Your neighborhood, ethnicity and life experiences are all designed to lead you to your destiny, to becoming you, to be who God called you to be.

Who is reading and studying your life right now? What are they learning from it? Maybe, you're living a successful life; you may have many accomplishments and even reached most of your goals. But I promise you until you receive Jesus Christ as your Lord and Savior and you're living holy, you are only living half if any of the life the Lord has for you. Am I saying that when you accept Jesus Christ as your Lord and Savior that you won't have any more problems, heartaches, pains or disappointments? Absolutely not! I believe the Word of God and here's what it says:

> *The righteous person faces many troubles, but the Lord comes to the rescue each time.* (Psalms 34:19 NLT)

You have received the grace, which was given to you to be saved.

> *For it is by grace you have been saved, through faith-and this is not from yourselves, it is the gift of God not by works, so that no one can boast.* (Ephesians 2:8-9 NIV)

The blessing in that is when you receive Jesus Christ as your Lord and Savior, you have faith and with that faith you are capable of pleasing God.

> *But without faith it is impossible to please him: for he that cometh to God must believe that he is, and that he is a rewarder of them that diligently seek him.* (Hebrews 11:6 KJV)

Can you imagine what life would be like for you if you please God who is in control of everything? Let me paint a picture for you to understand. It's like living in a kingdom and being a good friend or kin to the king himself. It does not mean you wouldn't ever experience sickness, poverty or disappointments. But what it does mean is that if and when you do, you have direct access to the king who has the means to treat your sickness, the means to change your state of poverty, and the means to take what you're disappointed about and give you what you wanted that's even better.

That's what it's like with God as your Father when you accept Jesus Christ as your Lord and Savior. Test, trials, problems, struggles, and disappointments in life will come, but God will always see you through them. He will develop a better you through them, which by the way is one of the main purposes for them.

> *Jesus spoke to the people once more and said, "I am the light of the world. If you follow me, you won't have to walk in darkness, because you will have the light that leads to life.* (John 8:12 NLT)

If that's not a clear enough picture, let's look further at what the Bible says God gives those who please Him.

> *God gives wisdom, knowledge, and joy to those who please him. But if a sinner becomes wealthy, God takes the wealth away and gives it to those who please him. This too, is meaning less – like chasing the wind.* (Ecclesiastes 2:26 NLT)

If ever you're discouraged, remember this important truth: Living holy is not about any right or wrong religion. Living holy is about living out your relationship with God to please Him. I believe it's safe to say that, the holier you live the closer you are to God. But I also want you to remember that as with any other relationship, you have to put in work to make it great. You can't just tell someone with your mouth, we are best friends or mates and never communicate or spend time with the person. The relationship will not thrive. So why treat your relationship with God that way? How do you treat your relationship with God that way? When you just receive Jesus Christ as your Lord and Savior and your relationship ends right there, where it began. It's great that you've received Him, but in order to develop a true relationship, you have to take the time to know Him by reading and studying God's Word, fasting, and praying.

For those of you who are thinking, "Well, I'm not ready for a relationship with God so if accepting Him isn't good enough, then I won't do that either. I'll just stay right here where I am." You had better get ready for your relationship with God because here's what God says to you:

> *Anyone who isn't with me opposes me, and anyone who isn't working with me is actually working against me.* (Luke 11:23 NLT)

I don't know about you but even if I did not know the Lord the way I know Him now, I would never want to be known to Him as being against Him. The choice is yours but know that you are mandated to live holy. You can't live your best life as God intended for you if you are unholy. My brothers and sisters, live holy! It's better than worth it. After all, it's the life you and everyone you've encountered have been waiting for you to live; to help fully appreciate this thing called life; through your authentic existence lived out in holiness!

> *I consider that our present sufferings are not worth comparing with the glory that will be revealed in us. For the creation waits in eager expectation for the children of God to be revealed. For the creation was subjected to frustration, not by its own choice, but by the will of the one who subjected it, in hope that the creation itself will be liberated from its bondage to decay and brought into the freedom and glory of the children of God.* (Romans 8:18-21 NIV)

My Prayer for You

My prayer for you is that if you never heard of or believed in God before reading this book that you now do. I pray that you will give God a try, challenge yourself to give Him your heart and believe in Him. I can't promise you every day will be sunshine; there will be some rainy days. The great men and women of the Bible, Christian's all over the world, Jesus Christ and I have all had difficult experiences. It may not seem like it while you're going through your storms of life but if you are in Christ Jesus, you already have the victory!

My prayer for the believers who read this book who have been living out your Christian journey on very bumpy roads under cloudy skies and blinding fog that prevents you from seeing ahead is that you have been encouraged. I pray that you will go back to the place where you first received the Lord when you had the passion, hunger, and thirst for Him and His purpose for your life. I pray that now that you have a better understanding of the life you are to live for Christ that you will live it out with focus, the fullness of joy, and no apologies.

I love you all my brothers and sisters and am praying for you. Please do the same for me as we are all in this together to uplift each other and God's kingdom and to destroy the Enemy and his! Let's remember to do so by living holy!

Chapter 10

PROMISES TO GOD'S CHILDREN

So shall my word be that goeth forth out of my mouth: it shall not return unto me void, but it shall accomplish that which I please, and it shall prosper in the thing whereto I sent it. (Isaiah 55:11 KJV)

You did not choose me, but I chose you and appointed you so that you might go and bear fruit —fruit that will last — and so that whatever you ask in my name the Father will give you. (John 15:16 NIV)

Truly I tell you, whatever you bind on earth will be bound in heaven, and whatever you loose on earth will be loosed in heaven. (Matthew 18:18 NIV)

You haven't done this before. Ask, using my name, and you will receive, and you will have abundant joy. (John 16:24 NLT)

Then you will call on me and come and pray to me, and I will listen to you. You will seek me and find me when you seek me with all your heart. (Jeremiah 29:12-13 NIV)

Call unto me, and I will answer thee, and shew thee great and mighty things, which thou knowest not. (Jeremiah 33:3 KJV)

You will pray to him, and he will hear you, and you will fulfill your vows to him. You will succeed in whatever you choose to do, and light will shine on the road ahead of you. (Job 22:27-28 NLT)

You can ask for anything in my name, and I will do it, so that the Son can bring glory to the Father. (John 14:13 NLT)

You can pray for anything, and if you have faith, you will receive it. (Matthew 21:22 NLT)

But if you remain in me and my words remain in you, you may ask for anything you want, and it will be granted! (John 15:7 NLT)

Again, truly I tell you that if two of you on earth agree about anything they ask for, it will be done for them by my Father in heaven. For where two or three gather in my name, there am I with them. (Matthew 18:19-20 NIV)

For every child of God defeats this evil world, and we achieve this victory through our faith. (1 John 5:4 NLT)

The Lord said to me, "You have seen correctly, for I am watching to see that my word is fulfilled." (Jeremiah 1:12 NIV)

The Lord says, "I will rescue those who love me. I will protect those who trust in my name. When they call on me, I will answer; I will be with them in trouble. I will rescue and honor them. I will reward them with a long life and give them my salvation." (Psalms 91:14-16 NLT)

But the Lord is faithful; he will strengthen you and guard you from the evil one. (2 Thessalonians 3:3 NLT)

I tell you the truth, those who listen to my message and believe in God who sent me have eternal life. They will never be condemned for their sins, but they have already passed from death into life. (John 5:24 NLT)

But if you look carefully into the perfect law that sets you free, and if you do what it says and don't forget what you heard, then God will bless you for doing it. (James 1:25 NLT)

I will answer them before they even call to me. While they are still talking about their needs, I will go ahead and answer their prayers! (Isaiah 65:24 NLT)

So do not throw away this confident trust in the Lord. Remember the great reward it brings you! Patient endurance is what you need now, so that you will continue to do God's will. Then you will receive all that he has promised. (Hebrews 10:35-36 NLT)

ACKNOWLEDGMENTS

First and foremost, I would like to thank and give honor to God for my life and for choosing me to birth this book through. Thank You Father for who You have made me to be and for how You are shaping and molding me into that wonderful God-fearing woman each and every day.

Thank you to my family for introducing me to Jesus Christ at such a young age and for giving me the privilege and honor to be brought up in a loving family where God is the center and foundation. Special thanks to my beautiful, anointed, and appointed Auntie Ida who was the only person I told about this book and who is always praying for me. Because of your prayers, encouragement, and the grace of God, this book has been birthed.

To my heaven sent Mama and friend Reina; who though I didn't tell about this book you've encouraged and loved me throughout the process of writing it more than you will ever know. Thank you for all of your love, support, and encouragement words can't express how grateful I am for you.

To my Auntie Dawn (Rev. Dr. Zavette D. Smallwood) thank you for your Pastoral leadership for a season of my life and for all of your preaching and teaching down through the years; which encouraged me in my Holiness. To all of the men and women of God throughout my life who have obeyed the Holy Spirit and have spoken words of prophecy over me, which encouraged me and helped me to believe, I say thank you. I wouldn't be who I am today if it were not for you. I love and appreciate you all. Thank you! I pray this book has blessed and encouraged you; to know that your prayers for me have not been in vain. Please continue to pray for me as I am certainly praying for you!

ABOUT THE AUTHOR

Juanita N. Stallings is an ambassador for Christ who not only believes in holiness but strives to practice it in her daily living. She loves and is in love with God (Jesus Christ), and has a burning desire for the world to know God, love God, and serve God as well! Juanita graduated from Mercy College where she received both her Bachelor's degree in Behavioral Science and her Master's degree in Counseling, graduating with distinction. Through her life experiences, she has developed a solid relationship with God and has learned how irrelevant denomination and church titles are and how very important salvation and one's heart are in God's eyes. Because of her love for God and His people, she's been burdened with a heart to know God in spirit and in truth and to share Him with the world, so they, too, can know, experience, and share God with the world!

www.ingramcontent.com/pod-product-compliance
Lightning Source LLC
LaVergne TN
LVHW051500070426
835507LV00022B/2857